TH1NK **REFERENCE COLLECTION**

history

THINK FOR YOURSELF ABOUT WHAT SHAPED THE CHURCH

Written by Robert Don Hughes

General Editor Karen Lee-Thorp

THINK

© 2008 by The Navigators

ISBN-10: 1-60006-137-0
ISBN-13: 978-1-60006-137-0

Cover design by Arvid Wallen
Creative Team: Nicci Hubert, Karen Lee-Thorp, Reagen Reed, Darla Hightower, Arvid Wallen, Matt Wallen, Kathy Guist

"About the TH1NK REFERENCE COLLECTION" by Mark Tabb

Unless otherwise identified, all Scripture quotations in this publication are taken from the *New King James Version* (NKJV). Copyright © 1982 by Thomas Nelson, Inc. Used by permission. All rights reserved. Other versions used include: the *New American Standard Bible* (NASB), © The Lockman Foundation 1960, 1962, 1963, 1968, 1971, 1972, 1973, 1975, 1977, 1995.

Library of Congress Cataloging-in-Publication Data

Hughes, Robert Don, 1949-
  History : think for yourself about what shaped the church / written by
Robert Don Hughes ; general editor, Karen Lee-Thorp.
     p. cm. -- (THINK reference collection)
  Includes bibliographical references.
  ISBN 978-1-60006-137-0
  1. Church history. I. Lee-Thorp, Karen. II. Title.
  BR145.3.H84 2008
  270--dc22

                                                  2007042128

Printed in the United States of America

1 2 3 4 5 6 7 8 9 10 / 12 11 10 09 08

This book is for you, Gail.
For your character, for your forgiveness, for your integrity,
for your faithfulness,
For your insight, for your laughter, for your love—
You are my anchor of faith, my rock of stability, my partner
in prayer,
My colleague upon the road, my daughter's mother,
My best friend, my soul mate, my wife.
Thank you for choosing to spend your life with me.

Contents

About the TH1NK Reference Collection 7

Introduction 9

1 Faithful unto Blood 19
  Polycarp

2 Heretical Fathers 39
  Tertullian and Origen

3 Fighting for Truth in the Imperial Church 61
  Constantine and Athanasius

4 Confession Is Good for the Church 83
  Augustine

5 Flames in the Darkness 103
  Patrick and the Early Middle Ages

6 Is There a Right Way to Know God? 123
  Francis and Aquinas

7 Faith Alone! Scripture Alone! Luther — Alone? 147
  Martin Luther

8 It's the Will of God! 161
  Calvin and Loyola

9 All English, All Certain 183
  Cranmer, Cromwell, and Bunyan

10 Moravians, Methodists, and Missions 207
    Von Zinzendorf, Carey, and Wesley

11 Awakening Faith, Awakening Conscience 229
    Revivalism, Millerism, and Christian Activism

12 The Explosive Twentieth Century........................... 249
    Liberalism, Mass Evangelism, and Pentecostalism

    Notes.. 273

    About the Author 275

About the TH1NK
REFERENCE COLLECTION

The TH1NK REFERENCE COLLECTION isn't an ordinary set of reference books. Like all of the books in the TH1NK line, we wrote these books for students. That doesn't mean we inserted some hip language into an otherwise dry, boring book to try to make it sound with-it and cool, dude. Instead, we built these books on a couple of assumptions about you.

First, we knew you want honest representations of various points of view. Although all the books in the REFERENCE COLLECTION are written from an evangelical Christian position, we didn't dismiss all other standpoints. Instead, we wrote these books in such a way that those holding different worldviews and theological perspectives would be able to read these books and say, *Yes, this gives a good outline of what I and others believe.*

We also believed you are able to draw your own conclusions. Whether the question regards what Buddhists believe or whether or not Christians can lose their salvation, we didn't connect all the dots for you. Each book presents several perspectives. You will have to take the next step on your own and figure out what you believe and why you believe it. Our goal is to do more than answer questions. The TH1NK REFERENCE COLLECTION is designed to make you think through your own beliefs and convictions, as well as those of others.

Finally, we assumed you want something more than a place to turn to for answers to your questions about Islam or Psalm

119 or the role of women in the church. That's why we designed these books to be read, not just researched. These are books you can read from cover to cover. Along the way, you will find that these books not only dispense information but also entertain you and challenge you and the way you see your world.

The NavPress TH1NK Team

Introduction

History. Yuck, right? Unpronounceable names that are even harder to spell. Pages of multiple-choice questions with date after date after date. Who can remember it all? Who would want to?

Of course, that's what happens whenever you have to learn what someone else wants you to know. But what about what *you* want to know?

Since you're reading this, I'm assuming you know and love Jesus—that you're a Christian. But what about the church? Do you love *it*? Or are there things about it that make you sick or make you mad? How did the church get to be like it is? It belongs to Christ Jesus, of course, but who made the critical decisions about what should be called orthodox theology? Who started the different denominations, and why are there so many splits?

Who made the choices that made the church what it is today? Somebody did. Or rather, lots of somebodies. And, yeah, some of them had unpronounceable names. But no matter how long ago or far away they lived, these people knew the same Jesus you know as Lord. They prayed each day to the same heavenly Father. They were filled with the same Holy Spirit you are. In fact, you have more in common with these brothers and sisters from the distant past than you do with many of the people you'll drive past today. They're part of your spiritual family tree, your Christian forebearers. The choices they made in their lives directly affect you. Some of those choices were positive, and some were really negative. What things about the church give you hope? What things about the church cause you to wonder if anybody in it knows what he's talking about? Why are some things so . . . wrong?

CAUSE AND EFFECT

The events that have made us the church are not just a muddle of bunched-up happenings that occurred for no reason. There's a sequence of cause and effect dating back to the beginnings of the church that explains *why* we Christians think the way we do—and why we don't all think the same. It's not a mystery; it's history. Understanding it will help you make better choices in your own life. And, if the Lord doesn't return for another thousand years, some of the choices you make might affect others just as much as did the decisions made long ago by the people we'll discuss.

Why this particular list of people? That's what makes history controversial. What I think is important may not be what you think is important. My selections might even irritate you. What if your favorite hero of the faith isn't on the list? That certainly doesn't mean that person hasn't influenced the kingdom of God. It just means that this is a short book and that I'm the gatekeeper of who and what we'll talk about. Given the opportunity to choose a few of the "most influential" figures in the history of the church, these are the ones that pop out at me. If this book does its job, you'll want to find out a lot more details anyway. There are many books filled with information on each of these figures—as well as many others of the "saints" we don't have space to mention.

HEROES?

I said "hero of the faith," didn't I? Were all of these people heroes? Not in the Hollywood sense, certainly. Most of them didn't plan to change the church — at least not in the ways that they eventually did. Most just tried to be faithful to the Word of God and recognized that the churches of their time didn't measure up to the ideal. That's still true of the church today, despite their best efforts. We all know that the churches in which we worship often fall short of the church that Jesus established. What can we do about it? Can we change bad patterns? We might want to model ourselves after some of the figures in this book. We might find ourselves in uncomfortable situations as we take stands that prove unpopular to people stuck in worldly practices. At least few of us risk being roasted alive for doing so!

Words like *reform*, *renew*, and *return* have described the goals of many of the great leaders of the church — especially those we'll examine. They lived in different ages, when different ways of thinking prevailed. In fact, we'll track the reality that the rules of logic and reason in one generation sometimes don't fly for later Christians. Does this mean the "faith which was once for all delivered to the saints" (Jude 3) *changes*? We know God doesn't change. Scripture doesn't change. But every generation interprets Scripture to understand God in the light of the time in which it lives. How *you* process information — any information, be it historical or theological or whatever — is different from the way Thomas Aquinas processed it, because he lived in a different time, in which people thought in different ways.

God birthed us into this day and age. We need to accept that reality and figure out how to help people process the gospel of Christ in the present. How do we know how to do that?

History can help. We can see how past generations responded to their own times with new *explanations* of the unchanging nature of God.

SIX BIG CHALLENGES

Six things jump out at me as I read church history — six challenges that show up again and again in the church no matter what the time or the place or the language used. Understanding these will help to explain why the church seems to be in need of reform in every generation. These will be our benchmarks as we (quickly) survey two thousand years of spiritual victories, human crises, and tragic false starts.

People Like Us

The first challenge is simply that the celebrated saints of church history were *people*. Imperfect people. They were, in fact, people like us. While this book is not designed to "dis" the greats of the church, it *is* going to try to be honest about the clay feet of those God has used. Only Jesus is perfect. The rest of us are just sinners saved by God's grace. If the saints of the past dealt with the same human problems we encounter daily, does that make them any less saintly — or us any more? Perhaps this will help us to be more honest about our own feet of clay and discourage us from trying to hide ourselves behind holy masks.

The Body of Christ and the Human Institution

The second challenge is that *we are dealing with something that is both the church of Christ and a human institution*. We know that Christ established his church and the gates of hell will not prevail against it. But that doesn't mean the powers of hell haven't established suburbs in certain pews. The book of Acts shows the church struggling with management issues. Acts 6 begins with complaints of one group against another group. The Holy Spirit guided the apostles to a solution of that issue, but it's clear that the church in Jerusalem was full of flawed individuals. Flawed individuals often find flawed solutions to problems, and as Acts continues we see more and more problems arising.

Look at the first few chapters of Revelation and you'll see that out of seven churches in Asia Minor, only two receive Christ's praise. Ephesus, the great mother church of all these, lost her first love (see 2:4). This expression may mean that the Ephesian church had gotten so tangled up in worldly concerns and local issues that the body of Christ was taking a back seat to the human institution. Similarly, churches today have one foot in God's world and the other foot firmly planted in earth's soil. Questions like, "Doesn't God want Christians to be rich?" and "Shouldn't we be giving more money to missions rather than adding on to the family center?" run across denominational lines. Every local body of genuine believers is part of the body of Christ, the church. But every local body is also an institution of flawed humans. If none of the ancient saints was totally righteous, how should we expect all church members to be? And church members—including pastors and leaders—are the people who fashion the institutions we call churches.

This is more than just another aspect of the "we're all just people" challenge. Sometimes very good people can build—or maintain—flawed, bad, even evil institutions. We'll talk about some of those flawed institutions, but let's be clear here: The church is simultaneously the body of Christ—in some ways his incarnate presence on earth—*and* a human institution.

In that way, the church is both holy and flawed. As we think through the centuries, we'll need to remind ourselves of this again and again. It's been a constant struggle in church history from the beginning.

Church + State = Very Bad Things

Which is a good place to move to the third challenge: *When the church gets married to the state, the result is very bad things.* After all, the church is the bride of Christ. It should be married only to the Lord. But since the time of Constantine, the church has again and again become so entangled in affairs of state that it has—yeah, I'll go ahead and use the word—*prostituted* itself. God used that image himself when talking of his people in Hosea.

Some have said that the church ought to be in *control* of the state. John Calvin, for example, believed this. Martin Luther may not have believed it originally, but he certainly wasn't a Christian revolutionary.

And what about those two words being used together: Is *Christian revolutionary* an oxymoron? One of the great criticisms the church has had to bear from the world is the historical record of how many people have been killed in Jesus' name—generally in support of or in revolution against the state. We'll try to see how the church has gotten entangled with the state in times past and look at whether that's a good idea or not.

Faith Versus Reason

A fourth challenge that recurs in almost every generation is *the primacy of faith versus reason.* This became especially pronounced in the years of the Enlightenment, when reason crowned science king and logic irrefutable. The fact of the matter is that most ideas are refutable, and we live in an age when science and logic have fallen under suspicion. The great irony of our postmodern time is how often logic is used to demonstrate how *nothing* is absolutely true.

Throughout Christian history there has been a constant plea from one quarter of the church or another to return to simple faith. But what does that mean, exactly? Each generation redefines simple faith in its own terms—in its own logic. While God doesn't change, and the biblical record remains available to all of us, the issue of faith versus reason changes like a kaleidoscope with every turn of the tube. There is a changing vogue of rationality in every age. This is why we have to become effective interpreters of the faith—and why old methods of doing this sometimes no longer work effectively.

What About Missions?

An interesting thing happened on the way to systematic theology. *Missions, which are the heart of the New Testament, got misplaced.* Up until Constantine in the fourth century, the church spread across the Roman world like a wildfire of evangelistic zeal. Then it slowed down to get organized. The great questions of Christology and Trinity were debated and resolved, which is good, but the church also got focused inward instead of outward. There were still missionaries, and they proved effective, but there were too few of them for too long. Marrying the Roman Empire didn't help. It meant that those outside the realm of Rome viewed Christianity as a Roman religion and a means of enslaving them. In some measure at least, that was true. Far to the north and east, the missionaries continued their activities, but often the nations that emerged in those new areas followed the Roman model of the state church—and missions were forgotten. Have missions been forgotten again in our present generation? Is that still a danger?

Ethics Optional?

Our final challenge—at least the last we'll consider closely —is *the tendency of some leaders to treat ethics as optional.* Some throughout history have been selective in the ethical standards they have lived by and/or taught. If the church has often been in bondage to the state, it has even more often been in bondage to the culture. The American church is not a state church—but it certainly is an *American* church.

Missions studies talk of the need for the church to become indigenous to the place in which it is planted, as a palm tree is indigenous to Hawaii and a redwood is to California. But these same studies warn of *accommodating* the gospel to the culture—changing the faith to fit the folks. This dilutes the gospel until it's no longer the gospel but something else. Nowhere does the level of accommodation of the church to its culture show up so starkly as in the ethical standards of its local Christians.

When this problem is really acute, we don't even recognize just how much the world's values have flavored our faith. While we may see this clearly in our present age, this is not a new problem at all. We can see people wrestling with these same issues back in—again—Acts. Does this mean we need to give up on ethics, rationalizing that what God really is concerned about is whether we've accepted Christ or not, and continuing to live exactly as the world does? I don't think that was the original idea—do you?

BACK TO BASICS

So what was the original idea? Reformers in every century have tried to get back to the New Testament model. Sometimes they've succeeded. Sometimes their successes have faded within a generation. Is it hopeless? Do we quit trying? Do we give up on the institutional church entirely and go out to live as hermits? (Actually, that's been tried, and it wasn't a silver bullet. It produced an institutional church composed of hermits.)

The joy of history is this: We can see that the problems we face are not new, even if they wear new faces. We can see that the faithful have never stopped struggling, even in the face of overwhelming odds. We can see that they made mistakes while they struggled, just as we do, yet God used them. Let's study the history of the church together through the lives of some of its best-known figures and pray that this study helps us to live just as courageously. And if the Lord doesn't return for another thousand years and our time becomes yet another chapter in the church's history, will those who come behind us find *us* faithful?

1

Faithful unto Blood

POLYCARP

The huge crowd that had gathered in the stadium of Smyrna stamped and roared and shouted for blood. Did the sun shine brightly on the carnage smeared across the dust of the stadium floor? Or did gray clouds slip sullenly across the sky, diffusing the light, cloaking the insanity of the crowd's hatred even from the enraged pagans themselves?

The Martyrdom of Polycarp doesn't tell us these details, but it does reveal many others: On a February day in AD 156, this angry mob had already watched eleven Christians from Philadelphia torn apart by lions. They had witnessed the bravery of young Germanicus, who'd refused to reject Christ and had instead pulled the hungry beasts to his chest. They had cackled in triumph as a Christian named Quintas quailed in terror and not only swore the oath to the emperor but also volunteered to betray Polycarp's hiding place to the authorities. Now they took up the chant, demanding that the aged leader of the church of Smyrna be caught and butchered. "Away with the atheists!" they screamed—meaning, of course, the Christians. Why did they think Christians were atheists?

Because Christians believed only in *their* God, not the Roman gods. "Let Polycarp be sought!" they shouted. And he was.

POLYCARP
ca. AD 70–156

Polycarp was a faithful leader of the church in Smyrna, whose life — although obscured by legend — appears to have stretched from the time of the apostles halfway into the second Christian century. Intent on delivering to following generations what he had received, he collected the letters of Ignatius, bishop of Antioch, who was martyred in Rome around 113, and may also have been an essential player in collecting the books that became the New Testament. Thought to have heard firsthand the testimony of the apostle John, he was the mentor of Iranaeus, one of the first great Christian apologists and bishop of Lyon. Polycarp's epistle to the Philippians is not very creative, but it certainly reflects his dependence on Scripture, for almost every line is a quotation from some earlier inspired work. Polycarp was martyred at the age of eighty-six, and his grace and peace in the face of the fire became a testimony to all the martyrs that followed him.

PASTOR POLYCARP

Yes, it's a funny-sounding name. I've never heard of anyone's naming a son after him. Why should this old pastor claim our attention? After all, others had been martyred before Polycarp, and *many* others have been since. We could as easily focus on Ignatius, the second bishop of Antioch, who wrote seven lengthy letters encouraging various churches as he traveled to

Rome to be killed. One of these was addressed to Polycarp, who was at that time the young pastor of Smyrna. In fact it was Polycarp who collected and preserved these letters so we can read them today. Or we could examine the life of Iranaeus, one of the first great apologists of the church, who defended the faith against the heresies of Marcion and the gnostics. Irenaeus, bishop of Lyon (in present-day France), had grown up in Smyrna under the teaching of—yes—Polycarp. While both Ignatius before him and Irenaeus after left lots of writings, history has preserved for us only one letter written by Polycarp. He sent it to the Corinthian church, and it reads like some term papers I've received from my students: a collection of quotations from the writings of others, strung together by *and*, *but*, and *so*. Some Christian scholars have even criticized Polycarp for being so unoriginal.

Perhaps that alone is a good enough reason to focus on this ancient pastor and teacher. He was in every way *orthodox*. That means he was faithful to pass along unchanged the message of the gospel as he received it—and he'd received it from the apostles themselves. One of his own mentors was John. Polycarp is a transitional figure in the life of the church—the last of those who had known the people who walked with the Lord, and the first of the leaders of the postapostolic age. We owe him a great deal for his faithfulness to the Word of God. He helped preserve it for us.

THE WITNESS OF JOHN

What must it have been like to sit and listen to the memories of "that disciple whom Jesus loved" (John 21:7)? John, after all, met Jesus on the day the Lord was baptized. He walked beside him for three years—saw him transfigured, crucified, and resurrected. John visited heaven and saw the whole of this history we study. He wrote the cosmic gospel and said at the end that if all the things Jesus did were written in detail, then the world itself couldn't contain all the books. But even if he couldn't write them all down, John surely remembered them. Imagine young Polycarp listening, his eyes and ears wide open, hearing details we'll not learn until we're in heaven ourselves.

He would have been a young man when John was taken at last to that glory that Revelation describes. Polycarp was born around AD 70, probably somewhere in Asia Minor (now Turkey) near the great city of Ephesus. Was he a second-generation Christian? It would seem so; when he died, he said he'd served God for eighty-six years. He missed seeing the man he called "the blessed Paul," but since Paul had planted the church in Ephesus and Smyrna was only about fifty miles away, he would have heard story after story about the great missionary from people who *had* known Paul. Timothy followed Paul as leader in Ephesus, and John followed Timothy. What a string of leaders that church had!

How the stories of the martyrs must have hung in Polycarp's mind. He lived, after all, with the threat of persecution all his life, beginning with those of Domitian (who became emperor in AD 81) on through to the persecutions of Antoninus Pius that finally took Polycarp's life. He knew those who had "resisted unto blood." Did he expect finally to become a martyr himself?

The Greek word from which we get *martyr* didn't originally mean a person who dies for a faith. It meant simply a "witness," as in a court of law. The word gained its more severe meaning in the Roman courts as Christians bore witness to their faith in Christ and thus condemned themselves to death.

John experienced the martyrdom of imprisonment on Patmos for his confession. But he survived and returned to Ephesus to share his vision.

Read John 21:18-23, and imagine what it must have been like for the believers when John died. They had all expected Christ to return before the last of the disciples passed from the scene, in part because of this incident. Did John's death cause a crisis of faith for young Polycarp? Probably. Don't we all tend to struggle when God doesn't meet our expectations? Whether he faltered or not, we can read the results of Polycarp's reaction to the beginning of the postapostolic period. He, with his friend Onesimus, became preservers of the written records that became the New Testament.

ONESIMUS OF EPHESUS

We know much about the prominent figures of the New Testament: Jesus, of course, and the disciples, as well as Stephen, Paul, Barnabas, Philip the Evangelist, James, Timothy, and John Mark. Others, like Epaphras and Philemon, we know much less about. Still others we know only by name and association with a particular church, as Paul greeted them at the end of one of his letters or Luke mentioned them in passing in the book of Acts. One of the intriguing characters about whom we know *some* is Onesimus. This is because Scripture includes a short personal letter from Paul to his friend Philemon regarding Philemon's runaway slave.

The name Onesimus meant useful, and in his letter Paul played upon that meaning as he explained to Philemon that his slave—who doubtless seemed useless since he'd run away—had been useful indeed to Paul during his imprisonment. Paul asked Philemon to accept back his servant and to treat him as he would Paul. Really, Paul demanded it of Philemon. We have to figure that Philemon did as Paul asked, because the letter has been preserved and included in Scripture. Why, exactly? Why would a personal letter regarding a slave be included with the great theological treatise of Romans and Paul's advice to the young pastors Timothy and Titus?

We're left to speculate on the answer to that because there is very little accurate information to go on beyond the New Testament books themselves. But there is record that a certain Onesimus became the bishop of the Ephesian church, guiding it at about the same time Polycarp led the church of Smyrna. (A bishop at this point in church history wasn't what we mean by bishop today. It was more the recognized leader of a number of associated house churches in an area.) It seems that Polycarp and Onesimus may have worked together to gather the writings we know as the New Testament. Would it be any surprise that the personal letter Onesimus delivered himself to his master would have been included by a grateful Onesimus? He knew firsthand that it was a genuine letter from Paul.

Ensuring that the writings of the New Testament were genuine was a major issue for the church in Polycarp's time. There were myriad documents floating about among the churches that claimed some connection to the apostles, many of these obviously fakes. Some of them put forward ideas that were absolutely contradictory to what we have come to know as Scripture. They come to light from time to time, and the media makes a big deal of them. Recently the so-called gospel of Judas was discovered, and naturally the media jumped to tell all about its "mysteries." Of course, the church knew of the gospel of Judas in the third century, dismissing it as a fake gospel filled with gnostic heresy. Good thing Polycarp was so insistent upon orthodox theology. The Roman world was as mixed up religiously as our own is today.

DOCETISM

Have you ever looked seriously at Scientology? This religion holds that the spirit is everything and the body is nothing. It's not a new idea. In the early years of the church, a number of groups made this same assumption, that all that counts is the spirit and the body is disposable trash. This type of thinking was part of what the New Testament writers were responding to when they emphasized the resurrection of Jesus' *body*, and the fact that Thomas could touch it. Some writers were already contending that what the disciples saw was a ghost. Others argued that Jesus had never been flesh and blood, but had only *appeared* to be. This is called Docetism (from the Greek word for "to seem, to appear").

Some odd ideas emerged from this kind of thinking. For instance, if your body is spiritually irrelevant, then you can indulge its appetites without worrying that your actions will affect your spirit. But if your body is as much "you" as your spirit is, and if Jesus dignified the human body by taking one himself, then what you do with and to your body (and other people's bodies) matters.

IGNATIUS

When Polycarp was still a young bishop, he was much influenced by his older friend Ignatius, who was fighting Docetism wherever he found it. Ignatius served as bishop of the church in Antioch, the first missionary church, which had sent out Barnabas and Paul. The fourth-century historian Eusebius said he became bishop in AD 69, just a few years after Paul's own martyrdom. He had been arrested late in the reign of Emperor Trajan (around 111–115) and was being taken to Rome to be fed to the wild beasts. As he traveled, he wrote letters to the churches of the Ephesians, the Magnesians, the Philadelphians, the Smyrnans, the Trallians, the Romans, and to Polycarp personally.

His writings show him to be a passionate man, almost neurotically obsessed with thoughts of how the wild beasts would tear him apart. He wrote to the Roman Christians to tell them that they were not to try to prevent his martyrdom. His other primary themes were loyalty and obedience to the local bishop (had he experienced frustrations with some of the lay leaders in Antioch?) and belief in Jesus' physical body. It was as if he saw his final legacy was to establish a legitimate chain of authority in the church to combat false teachings.

Polycarp made a point of collecting and preserving Ignatius' letters and thereby picked up the crusade against distorted teaching. One certain way to combat toxic teaching was to ensure that the faith "once and for all delivered to the saints" would be preserved in written form.

GNOSTIC HERESIES

Preserving the integrity of the books that would become the New Testament became critical in Polycarp's generation, because gnostic teachers were mixing the teaching of the apostles with other, contradictory elements. *Gnosis* is Greek for "knowledge," and the various gnostic groups taught that they had special, inside knowledge on Jesus that the Christian churches didn't have. (Sounds a bit like *The Da Vinci Code*, doesn't it? It should. This is where all those "secret teachings" got started.) Groups like these had already begun in

Paul's day, but they became bolder once the apostles had all died. Their theologies varied, but all seemed to agree that the material world was not important—only the spiritual world mattered. They hated the physical body and elevated the spirit in two fairly simple equations: body = bad, spirit = good. Who were these people, and how did they come to have so much influence?

Some groups are referred to as Judeo-gnostics: These sects, including the Ebionites, Elkesaites, Sabians, and Mandaeans, all appeared in the first century. They emerged from a Jewish background and held to the Torah (the Law of Moses), but had a much more Greek-philosophical understanding of Judaism than did the rabbis or the temple priests. They all had differing views of Jesus, but while each believed him to be the Messiah, they did not view him as the Son of God. They denied the crucifixion and held that Jesus and Satan had been begotten of God together. Some aspects of present-day Mormonism appear to be echoes of this ancient view.

Simon Magus, Menander, Satornilus, and Basilides were all Samaritan gnostics who were linked together by their Samaritan tribal heritage and (to some extent) succeeded one another. Simon Magus is mentioned in Acts 8:18 as seeking to buy the power of the Holy Spirit. A widely known magician in the first century, he passed to his disciples a belief that redemption was not by faith alone but by transcendental magic. This "secret knowledge" was passed along only to those who *deserved* to hear it.

Then there were Cerinthus and Carpocrates, Jewish-Christian gnostics who taught in Alexandria, Egypt. They believed that Jesus was just an ordinary man who received the "Christ force" at his baptism, which then departed from him before the crucifixion. Polycarp's student Irenaeus said that John wrote his gospel to refute Cerinthus. That helps us to understand the stress John placed upon "the Word became *flesh* and dwelt among us" (1:14, emphasis added) doesn't it?

Carpocrates claimed to possess secret teachings disclosed by Jesus to his apostles, and he used a secret gospel, allegedly written by John Mark, which contained erotic rites. Sex and sin were to be encouraged since they highlighted God's grace. What? It's like this: If you want to receive a lot of grace, then sin *grandly.* Some scholars think this was the same teaching practiced by the Nicolaitans, a group condemned in Revelation 2:15.

But the most influential of the second-century gnostics was Valentinus. He left the Roman church when he was not made the bishop. We can quickly see why he wasn't: He taught that God gave rise to eight emanations, which produced in turn fifteen male-female pairs of angelic beings, which through their sexual activities procreated the material cosmos. Valentinus urged his followers to emulate the actions of these angelic pairs. An important Valentinian orgiastic celebration began on the evening preceding the Roman Lupercalia—that is, on February 14. (Does that date sound familiar? Something about *Valentine's* Day?)

All of these groups and ideas were afloat in the Roman world during the second century, and Polycarp struggled to maintain orthodox beliefs in the face of their influence. He had a face-to-face encounter with another former Christian named Marcion, who taught that only the soul is the object of redemption—not the body. The Marcionite sect became one of the greatest challenges to the early church, forcing it to establish the biblical canon in defense against his teachings.

A rich shipbuilder and the son of a Christian bishop, Marcion arrived in Rome around AD 140 and began to study gnostic teachings. He developed his own ideas about Jesus and spread them to others. He didn't believe Jesus had ever been a flesh-and-blood man. In Marcion's view, Jesus had been a spirit that *looked* like a man. Jesus wasn't born; rather, he suddenly appeared in AD 29 in the synagogue at Capernaum. While Marcion argued that Christ's life and crucifixion were necessary, he didn't believe Christ actually suffered or died on the cross. Nor did he believe in the resurrection of the body. This is, again, Docetism.

It's worth remembering this idea, for there are people today whose view of Christ is similar, and who have little interest in the physical world. After all, flesh is evil, right? While other sects moved toward free sexuality in defiance of legalism, Marcion taught a strict asceticism (that means denying the body) that forbade relations even between married couples. The end was coming soon, he said, and they needed to keep themselves spiritually pure. This idea has shown up again and again through the centuries. The Shakers of the 1800s practiced it—which is why they died out. The Heaven's Gate cult that committed group suicide in 1997 held the same view.

Marcion despised the Jews and the God of the Old Testament. He said Christianity was a gospel of love and not law, and that when Christ descended into hell Cain, Esau, and the men of Sodom all accepted his message. Abel, Enoch, Noah, and the Jewish patriarchs did not and therefore remained below. All of the New Testament books had been written by this time, and Marcion had a collection of them, but he put together a version of his own in which he edited out what he didn't like. Whatever sounded too Jewish to him, he discarded. He threw away all the gospels except that of Luke, and he cut the birth story out of *it*. He also cut out Acts, the pastoral letters, Revelation, and Hebrews, keeping only ten of Paul's letters. He believed Paul was the only apostle who did not corrupt the gospel of Jesus. Of course, through his editing, he pretty well corrupted Paul's teachings too.

Marcion's ideas were roundly rejected by the church at Rome, and it tossed him out in 144. This didn't stop him. Like many a present-day cult leader, he set up his own organizations which he called churches and thereby drew away many followers of Christ.

This was the heretic Polycarp met face-to-face. Irenaeus wrote that when Polycarp ran into Marcion one day in the street, Marcion asked Polycarp, "Do you recognize me?"

"Indeed!" Polycarp responded, pulling away. "I recognize you as the firstborn of Satan!"

Polycarp was a straight speaker—perhaps even a bit tart tongued—but he said what he believed. You can see that in his response to Marcion, which is echoed in his letter to the Philippians (see "Polycarp to the Philippians" 7:1). In that same letter, he rebuked Valens (about whom we really only know this), saying, "I am very unhappy on account of Valens, who was formerly made an elder among you, that he should so misunderstand the office given him. I exhort you, then, to abstain from love of money and to be pure and trustworthy" (11:1). Was it his sharp tongue and his unwillingness to speak anything but the truth that got him into trouble that day in the arena?

Let us persevere then constantly in our hope and the pledge of our righteousness, which is Christ Jesus, who bore our sins in his own body on the cross, who did no sin, nor was any deceit found in his mouth, but endured all things for us that we might live in him. Let us be imitators, then, of his endurance, and if we suffer for his name let us glorify him. For this is the example which he set in himself, and this we learned to believe.

"POLYCARP TO THE PHILIPPIANS" 8:1-13

UNSOUGHT MARTYRDOM

A new persecution, mostly local in nature, threatened the church in Smyrna. Polycarp was old, and he didn't want to run from it, but, like Paul in Acts 19:30-31, he agreed to his friends' requests and allowed himself to be hidden. He was in a farmhouse on the outskirts of the city when the authorities, directed to the place with the help of the turncoat Quintas, finally found him. Unruffled by their rough treatment, he offered them dinner and asked permission to pray while they ate. He prayed for about two hours, and those who had come to arrest him began to feel bad that they had to apprehend such a godly old man.

Polycarp was unsurprised by these events. He'd had a vision in a dream several days earlier, in which his pillow had caught fire, and when he awoke he told those who were hiding him that he knew he would be burned alive. The arresting officers pleaded with him to respect his age and simply say, "Caesar is Lord." He would not, so they took him back to the stadium, still filled with people roaring for his blood. The proconsul begged him to change his mind and to say, "Away with the atheists!" — meaning the Christians. Polycarp instead looked at the crowd, waved his hands dismissively at them, and cried up to heaven, "Away with the atheists!" — meaning *them*.

The proconsul tried again: "Take the oath and I will let you go. Revile Christ." Polycarp answered, "I have served him eighty-six years, and in no way has he dealt unjustly with me, so how can I blaspheme my king who saved me?"

Frustrated, the proconsul threatened him with wild beasts. Polycarp said, "Bring them on." Was he thinking of the death of his friend Ignatius when he said this? Then the proconsul threatened to burn him to death. Here was the fulfillment of his vision. Polycarp answered, "You threaten me with fire, which burns for an hour and is soon quenched. But you are ignorant of the fire of the coming judgment and eternal punishment reserved for the wicked. But why do you wait? Come, do what you will!"

There was no firewood in the stadium, but the mob ran out into the nearby shops and collected wood of every kind to burn him. Soon a pyre was made. Why were they so angry? Why were they so violent? Why were they so intent on destroying the witness of this one old man? Was it because they saw their way of life disappearing into the fires of the persecutions, as more and more people around them accepted the gospel and let it change their lives? As for destroying Polycarp's witness — well, they didn't, after all. We're talking about him still. We have the story of his witness — his martyrdom — still today.

Those who wrote of the event testified of miracles — that the fire couldn't consume his body, that it instead arched above him like a sail. In an echo of the Crucifixion, he was then stabbed in the chest — and a dove ascended into heaven even as his blood spilled out and doused the fire. Shall we believe these accounts? Those who watched testified to it, and the story spread widely through the Roman world. Miracles do happen when God so chooses. Once Polycarp was dead, the Jews present urged the proconsul to burn his body so there would be no threat of resurrection stories as well. The faithful collected his bones—"more precious than costly stones and finer than gold"—and kept them in a safe place. From that day on they celebrated this "birthday" with joy, remembering Polycarp and the Lord he'd glorified to the very end. They wrote, "Through patience he overcame the unjust magistrate and thus carried off the crown of incorruption, and rejoicing with the apostles and all the just he is glorifying God and the Father Almighty and is blessing our Lord Jesus Christ, the Savior of our souls" (*The Martyrdom of Polycarp* 19:2).

The account of Polycarp's martyrdom set the pattern for a new form of Christian literature, the martyrdom story. Many other such accounts followed, from those of Justin Martyr, Irenaeus, and women like Perpetua in these early centuries, to *Foxe's Book of Martyrs* in the sixteenth century, to the recent martyrdom stories of Bill Wallace and Jim Eliot. These stories have inspired Christians of every generation to "resist unto blood" and to carry the gospel everywhere regardless of the personal cost. If, after Jesus, Peter, Paul, and others, Polycarp's courage helped to establish this pattern, then certainly he made a lasting impact on the church. But was that impact altogether positive? Let's think through our six points:

People Like Us

Polycarp was certainly a man of flesh and blood—a person like us. But the story of his martyrdom is less an account of a normal Christian saint and more the veneration of a completely holy Saint (note the capital *S*). It was the herald of a problem that would grow. *The Martyrdom of Polycarp* is what is referred to as hagiography, or "writings of the holy." This kind of writing separates the Saints from ordinary Christians, and in some way makes them seem different from us. In that difference we can find excuses for ourselves. We, after all, are not Saints—but ordinary saints. The standards, then, need not be so high for us. But that's not true, is it, if these people we study were people like us?

The saving of Polycarp's burned bones encouraged the veneration of "relics"—pieces of the bodies of the Saints that came to be almost—or literally—worshipped by later Christians. We'll see later that Martin Luther had plenty to say about this. Why would people venerate a Saint? Start with the belief that there are some heroic Christians who deserve to be remembered for the example they set. Today, for instance, there are celebrity Christian leaders on radio or television, or who write books that millions read, or who pastor huge churches, and lots of believers look up to them. There's nothing wrong with that unless our tendency to idolize the famous gets out of hand. And sometimes it does get out hand. Heroes—role models we want to listen to and imitate—are a good thing. Hero *worship* can be a problem.

Next, add the entirely orthodox belief that Christians who have died still live eternally, and one day we'll all be together with Christ. So if it's appropriate to ask a Christian friend to pray for you when you're struggling with something, and if it would be great to ask a real giant of the faith to pray for you, then what about asking a giant of the faith who no longer lives on this earth? Many Christians today would say there's nothing in the Bible about doing that, so it's going too far. But in Polycarp's time, it started happening, and it became common in later centuries. Roman Catholics and Eastern Orthodox still do this, and they don't consider it worship of the Saint or an occult practice. What do you think?

Then add the fact that humans naturally respect the physical remains of their beloved dead. Today a lot of people bury their loved ones in wildly expensive caskets designed to keep air out so the body won't quickly decompose. So treating the bones of a dead believer with respect makes sense. But how far do you go in treating remains with respect? Today it's a hermetically sealed titanium casket for one's mother; in the Middle Ages it was jeweled boxes for bones of the Saints. And then there grew up a thriving business in the sale of supposed remains of Saints. And if miracles happened to Polycarp when he was dying, why not miracles connected to his remains? A faith in God's ability and willingness to intervene in our world to display his glory can easily slip into a belief in magic. If you watch enough Christian television today, you'll hear things that sound a bit more like magic than like biblical faith.

It's incredibly easy for something that starts sensibly to get out of control—and many Protestants feel that veneration of the Saints got way out of control and needed to be changed or eliminated entirely. One reason to study the church's history is to see how things got extreme in the past so you'll notice if something similar is happening to you.

The Body of Christ and the Human Institution
Throughout this period, we can witness the growth of the church as an institution—a necessary growth in response to heresy and to organizational instability. But there was also

a fairly constant emphasis in the writings of the period on maintaining the church as the body of Christ. Collecting the canonical writings helped to network together the like-minded, provided a shared record of the past, and set a standard against which to measure new — and contrary — teachings. Ignatius's emphasis on the pastoral authority of bishops was certainly well intentioned. Still, when an organization becomes an institution, its original purpose often becomes captive to the health of the organization. The seeds were being sown for the growth of a hierarchy that could be diverted from its primary cause.

Church + State = Very Bad Things

In contrast to the gnostics and others who wanted to subtract aspects of the gospel, the Bible, or Jesus' identity, the church in this period began to call itself *catholic*, meaning "the whole thing." The word *catholic* was used first by Ignatius in his letter to Smyrna (shortly after AD 100), and then appears three times in *The Martyrdom of Polycarp*. It wasn't applied to a particular *part* of the church until much later.

This catholic church lived in defiance of the Roman state, so it was not yet influenced by the state negatively, apart from persecution. The growing list of martyrs was instead having a positive effect — the pagan Roman world was beginning to admire the courage of Christians.

Faith Versus Reason

How did reason relate to faith during this period? Certainly a type of "reason" drove much of the gnostic reaction to the faith. Gnosticism showed the imprint of Greek philosophy — especially that of Plato — mixed with "mystery" religions of the day that melded Egyptian, Babylonian, and Hindu elements.

It was this same Greek-flavored reason that was to bend the thinking of Origen in the next century, which we'll talk about in the next chapter. Meanwhile, faith remained central to the Christian response to gnostic and Marcionite attacks.

What About Missions?

The missionary purpose of the church was still ever-present, with martyrdoms serving as a powerful (if unintentional) means of publicizing the gospel.

Ethics Optional?

Ethics were far from optional in this period, and the way men and women like Polycarp lived out the principles of holiness attracted attention from non-Christians. Now there *were* some ethical debates peculiar to the period: Quintas, who had volunteered for martyrdom but changed his mind when he saw the beasts, caused the church to regard *seeking* martyrdom as unethical. But there were also growing debates among Christians about whether it was ethical to *flee* martyrdom. This question would cause a rift in the church in the next generation. But whatever the ethical impact of these questions in a time of persecution, there can be no doubt that it was the morality and holiness of Christians that brought them under this persecution in the first place. Christians were different. They lived differently—so differently that they challenged the pervasive immorality of the age. Which raises the question for Christians in *our* age: Can the world see such a difference in *us*?

WANT TO KNOW MORE?

Many books are available concerning the postapostolic fathers, but the best resources are probably the writings of the Fathers themselves. Jack Sparks's *The Apostolic Fathers* (Nashville: Thomas Nelson, 1997) is excellent. Besides the section on Polycarp, you can read there the letters of Clement and Ignatius, as well as the *Didache*, *The Shepherd of Hermas*, and the so-called *Letter of Barnabas*. These are not Scripture, although they were highly regarded well into the third century. However, they provide for us a window to a period of history most Christians know little about, the age closest to the apostles themselves.

2

Heretical Fathers

TERTULLIAN AND ORIGEN

About the time Polycarp was burned, a baby was born into a military family in North Africa. Fifteen or twenty years later, another baby was born in North Africa to the family of a new convert to Christianity. The first was raised in Carthage in a thoroughly Roman-ruled environment. The other grew up in Alexandria, the second most important city in the Roman world but wholly Greek in its outlook. While both men became proficient in Latin and Greek, the man from Carthage became the "Father of Latin Theology" and provided the lasting definition of the Trinity. The other became a philosopher-theologian who helped mesh the Greek mindset of Plato and Aristotle with a spiritual understanding of the gospel. He is easily called the "Father of Greek Theology."

Both wrote compelling works of apologetics, defending the Christian faith against the attacks of pagan writers. The man in the West (Carthage), a lawyer by training, became steadily harder-edged and more legalistic in his thinking and writing. The man in the East (Alexandria) grew more speculative, more metaphysical in his thinking, more . . . fuzzy. The western writer was brittle and caustic, using his legal language and brilliant phrasing to slash his opponents and shred their arguments. The eastern theologian wrote from his heart as much as from his head, pouring out a deluge of writings that probed high into the heavens and deep into the heart of God. The Carthaginian appears rather unlikable. The Alexandrian seems thoroughly lovable. And while, between the two, they gave to the church its most foundational theological works, neither was made a saint. In fact, both are regarded today as having strayed into heresy. The western writer was Tertullian. The eastern theologian was Origen.

HERESY?

Heretic! The word means the holder of an unorthodox opinion, belief, or practice that is contrary to the accepted biblical doctrine of the church. *Orthodox*, by the way, means the commonly accepted or "true" doctrine. Which raises the question "accepted by *whom*?" We live in a time when there are many different Christian denominations, many of which see certain beliefs of others as heresy. Obviously, we need to be really careful with such a land-mine word.

But the period we're talking about here was a time when Christians felt it was important to get clear on what the *whole* Christian faith was and what was so far afield that it *wasn't* the gospel. The goal wasn't uniformity—in this period, churches in Syria still did things very differently from churches in Rome, and that was okay. Rather, the goal was to identify what diversity was still under the tent of the apostles' teaching and what lay outside that tent. Christian leaders wanted to say, "That road there is a detour, and if you go far enough down it, you'll hit a dead end. We've thought it through, and here's why we think what we do." But, as seems inevitable with humans, the emotions of various leaders ran high and people began calling each other heretics—and worse.

Why read about heretics when we're trying to think deeply about the history of the orthodox Christian faith? Tertullian and Origen wrote in a day before church leaders had thought (and argued!) through what the Bible taught on a variety of issues, such as: "What does it mean to say that Jesus Christ is both God and man? What does that do to monotheism?" Tertullian and Origen were in the first generation that could thoroughly read the whole of the Old and New Testaments, as well as other writings preserved by Onesimus, Polycarp, and others, and try to make sense of both the clear declarations and the apparent contradictions they found there. (Remember that books were copied by hand in those days, so before Polycarp got to work, a given church might own some of Paul's letters but not all of them, and Luke's gospel but not John's.)

The "canon" of Scripture (that means the books everybody agreed were genuine writings of the apostles, worth reading and memorizing) was not yet completely fixed. There were books that were widely circulated that would later be discarded— Jewish books like the visions of Enoch, or *The Shepherd of Hermas*, which many Christians thought Barnabas had written. There were books familiar to us—such as Hebrews and Revelation—that were highly valued by some but rejected by others. There were still other books, like the gospel of Thomas or the gospel of Judas, which gnostics liked but Christian theologians rejected with disgust. Who had the last say on what was orthodox or not? Who could decide who was a heretic?

Apparently, anyone could. The charges of heresy flew fast and furious between churches and between regions of the empire. The East, including what is now Greece, Turkey, Syria,

Egypt, and so on, primarily used the Greek language. This language was rich in words that had been charged with meanings by the great philosophers of Athens and elsewhere. The same word could be taken many different ways—and was. In the West, along the Italian peninsula and western North Africa, the Latin language predominated. While the Greeks were thinkers, the Romans were doers, and their language (especially their legal language) reflected practicality and precision. There are strong arguments in linguistics that say the language you use affects the way you *think*, and certainly the western and eastern churches thought differently. And to some people, thinking differently meant somebody *must* be thinking heretically.

Another dynamic also led to charges of "Heresy!" and "Anathema!" (That latter word means to curse someone or something and to refuse to have anything to do with that detested person or object.) Despite continuing persecutions, churches were growing richer. New Christians kept coming into the church and contributing financially to the organization. At the same time, the church's growth subtracted adherents and money from the pagan temples and the mystery cults. With wealth comes power, and with power, jealousy—and various forms of corruption soon follow after.

I guess we could say, "*Newsflash! This just in: Satan is at work inside churches!*" While this is often—no, always—a shock to new believers, it is not a new thing. To many Christians in the Roman Empire of the 200s, some churches had departed from the simple gospel of Jesus almost from the time of the apostles themselves. What a convenient tool declaring your political enemies "Heretics!" and "Anathema!" became.

Into this confused picture of honest piety and corrupt

power-thirst, Tertullian and Origen tried to insert some order and logic. The fact that they were different personalities from different worlds of thought led them to different explanations of the Christian faith, and to different conclusions. But if you read them both—at least if you read their best, most constructive writings—you'll find two men earnestly contending for the faith of Christ Jesus and earnestly loving God. And yes, both of them *were* heretics, at least at points.

TERTULLIAN'S LIFE

TERTULLIAN (QUINTUS SEPTIMIUS FLORENS TERTULLIANUS)
ca. 155–230

A Latin lawyer born in Carthage, North Africa, Tertullian wrote so prolifically and effectively on the Christian faith that he became known as the "Father of Latin Theology." Converted in middle age, Tertullian applied his jurist's training both to exposition of the Scriptures and the defense of Christianity.

As he grew older, he became more narrow and legalistic in his perceptions of Christian living, until he became stricter than most bishops and left the church in disgust. He first joined the Montanists, an early eschatological cult. Then, determining they weren't severe enough, he formed his own cult, the Tertullianists, which survived into the fifth century.

He was the first Christian writer to use the term *Trinity* and to coin the concept of God as "one substance, three persons." He also coined the terms *New Testament* and *Old Testament*. His writings had great impact on the church in the Western Empire generally, and specifically on Augustine.

We really don't know much about Tertullian's life — just some facts gleaned from his own writings and some later writers' comments. It appears that he was born in North Africa, probably in Carthage. His father was a Roman centurion, and there is no record that his family had anything to do with Christianity. In fact, it seems he joined with others in mocking Christianity until he reached midlife. He was a trained lawyer, and his life up until his conversion was one of sin and self-indulgence. But somewhere in his forties he experienced a transformation. His experience made him unable to imagine a truly Christian life without a conscious, radical breach with the past. He said in his *Apologeticum* that Christians are "made, not born." He came to a passionate, lasting, and legalistic faith in Christ Jesus, and turned his lawyer's expertise and obvious brilliance to defending the faith he had scorned.

Somewhere around 197 he burst onto the landscape of Christian thinking with "To the Martyrs," "To the Nations," and "Apologeticum." If we can learn anything of his personality from his writing style, it is that he was both bright and brittle, sharp and sarcastic. This will show up more as we talk about his best lines. Some writers believe he became a presbyter (a nonordained lay leader) in Carthage. Others believe he spent the middle part of his life in Rome and became a presbyter in that great church. Wherever he was, he certainly demonstrated his learning in his writings. He knew the heresies of Marcion and Valentinus in detail — and both of these gnostic teachers are associated with the Roman church. He was the first theologian to write in Latin, and he provided the church with legal language that became helpful in the controversies of the next generation. But while he continued to write and publish for about twenty years, he formally left the church around 211, and for the last five years of that time he was attached to an extremist movement within the church, the Montanists.

MONTANISM

There are, unfortunately, a number of early Christian heresies whose names begin with *m*. This one is named for its founder, Montanus, who really only wanted to see the church return to its early emphasis on the Holy Spirit and the Second Coming. He saw the growing power of the bishops and the church organization, and the correspondingly decreasing emphasis on spontaneity. In other words, he was another church reformer. Perhaps he'd still be viewed as such if he hadn't gone the direction of so many reformers and moved to the other extreme.

He started his crusade in western Turkey and was soon joined by two prophetesses. They spoke in tongues and prophesied the immediate return of Jesus. Emphasizing the continuing revelation of the Holy Spirit, they overemphasized direct revelation in a time when the church as a whole was struggling to resolve the issue of what should and should not be considered Scripture. Eventually Montanus was calling himself "the Paraclete" and giving dates and places where the Second Coming would take place (see, none of this is original to the twenty-first century!). When the predictions didn't come true, the Montanists accused the larger church of failing to receive the blessing because of its moral laxity.

It was probably their asceticism that most attracted Tertullian. They proclaimed that marital relations were to be abandoned—chastity was to be the rule until Jesus returned. There should be no remarriage after the death of a spouse. The number of fast days should be multiplied, and only dry food should be eaten. The Christian should never run from persecution but should suffer martyrdom gladly as God's will. There were sins that were unforgivable after baptism—sins that no amount of repentance and restitution could set right.

These views apparently appealed to Tertullian's legalistic mind. As he grew older, his strictness and intolerance grew. Like a crotchety old man who stands around criticizing the behaviors of everyone—especially the young—Tertullian found more and more to dislike in Christians. He scorned bishops who received back into the flock Christians who had strayed, arguing that this eroded discipline in the churches. He insisted that remarriage after a spouse's death was sinful and wrote *two* books to his wife to tell her how much of a sinner she would be if she remarried after his death. He believed virgins should constantly be veiled. (He was neither the first nor the last man to think women's faces rather than men's heads were the cause of lust.)

We don't know whether he left the church voluntarily or was forced out. Perhaps he left when the other Montanists were being pushed out. Perhaps he was fired as a presbyter by bishops he had attacked for being too lax in discipline. Some say he left the church of Rome and went home to Carthage in anger. Others said he'd never left Carthage—just the church. Whatever the reason, once he left, he wrote diatribes against the churches even more poisonous than those he'd fired at the pagans and the heretics.

We also know that eventually even the Montanists disappointed him with their lack of discipline. He had been leading a small Montanist congregation in Carthage. He left it and started his own "denomination," which became known as the Tertullianists. Two hundred years later, Augustine helped these congregations rejoin the church.

For throughout his judgmental tirades, Tertullian maintained his firm faith in Jesus Christ. That was never in question. Jerome said that he lived to an extreme old age (we don't know if his wife survived him to remarry). And while he never relented and begged to be readmitted to the church (as Marcion apparently did), Tertullian had already bequeathed to the church theological thought and language that would become essential to all of us who have come after him. "Like what?" you might ask. How about his spelling out of the concept of the Trinity, based on exhaustive study of the Scriptures?

TERTULLIAN'S BEST LINES

Despite his temperamental personality and self-righteous attitude, Tertullian has often been quoted. That's probably because of his pithy, pungent writing style. He could say with a sentence what other writers needed paragraphs to convey. So instead of listing his writings, let's look at some of his best lines.

One of the most quoted is the statement, "The blood of the martyrs is seed." Most of the time, people add "of the church," because that's what he meant. Tertullian was saying that every time the Roman government spilled the blood of Christians, more Christians sprang up to take the place of those killed. This was a true observation for his time. (And in many places around the world it remains so today.) Many citizens of the empire were growing weary of watching Christians killed for nothing more than worshipping their God. The martyrdom (which means witness, remember?) of believers caused non-Christians to examine their own values and religions and prompted many to ask questions about the faith. This may have been part of the reason why the attacks on Christianity—both through physical violence and through the written word—grew more savage.

With debater's skills honed in the Roman courts of law, Tertullian turned the words of the attackers against them: "'See,' they exclaim, 'how they [Christians] love one another?'" he wrote sarcastically, quoting them. Christian love was no vice to be suspected and feared, but rather a virtue of honest faith. He argued, "The soul is by nature Christian." Here he meant that all people have a longing for the truth of God.

At times he could be unfair in his debating (he was, after all, a trained lawyer). Another of his most famous quotes is, "What has Athens to do with Jerusalem?" In other words, the truth of the Christ who was crucified in Jerusalem could not be approached by the reasoning of the Athenian philosophers, for it was on another plane entirely. Faith = good; philosophy = bad. But in fact Tertullian often made use of philosophical constructs in his own arguments—and even affected the clothing style of the philosophers, identifying himself with them. Still, the statement draws amens in Christian classrooms today from students weary of trying to understand human reasoning and wanting an excuse to discard it entirely. Tertullian didn't do that, and if we were to do it today we would lose the opportunity to make any impact on our world. Still, it's a great line.

Perhaps his greatest linguistic contributions to the faith, however, were his theological terms. He was the first to describe the Hebrew Scriptures written prior to Jesus as the "Old Testament" and the Greek Scriptures written after Jesus as the "New Testament." And it was his framing of the nature of God as "one substance, three persons" that eventually won the day in the confusing debates that raged later concerning the relationship of Father, Son, and Holy Spirit.

Perhaps he was a mean-spirited, judgmental old sourpuss. But we owe this man honor. He influenced the faith we share today, whether he seems likable or not. His overall positive contributions to Christianity outweigh his late-in-life stubbornness. I'm not certain we can say that about his contemporary in the East—even though Origen seems to be a much more engaging personality.

ORIGEN'S LIFE

ORIGEN (ORIGENES ADAMANTIOS)
ca. 184–ca. 254

A brilliant second-generation Christian of the Greek-cultured city of Alexandria, Egypt, Origen became the teacher of the Alexandrian School (of theology) at eighteen. Following the lead of his teacher and predecessor, Clement, he incorporated Platonic thought into the Christian faith so that the intellectuals of the Eastern Roman Empire could understand Christianity. He was a thorough-going Platonic idealist, which meant that he regarded the spiritual world as far more meaningful than the practical world, the "ideal" world more solid than the world of matter.

This view caused Origen to move into metaphysical speculations that went beyond the revelation of Scripture. He introduced the concept that the Scriptures should be read on three levels — the literal, the moral, and the allegorical. Caught in the crossfire of church politics, he left Alexandria and moved to Caesarea, where he wrote and taught so prolifically and creatively that he became a trusted source for resolving theological disputes.

Tortured during the persecution of Decius, he survived to the age of sixty-nine and died surrounded by those who had come to love him. While he became the father of Greek theology, some of his ideas contributed to the growth of a heresy called Arianism, and three hundred years after his death, the church officially declared him a heretic.

Origen's father had been his teacher, his coach, and his model—and he'd been martyred. And at just sixteen, Origen was ready to follow in his father's footsteps and present himself for martyrdom to the Roman authorities in Alexandria. Problem was, he couldn't find his clothes. His mother, guessing his intent (or did he tell her?), had hidden them. He couldn't very well walk out of the house naked—and as a result one of the greatest minds of the early church was preserved to write—and write and write.

Obviously passionate and devoted to Christ, Origen turned his attention to expanding his faith through education. His father had already taught him much—so much that he was qualified to teach subjects like geometry and literature as well as theology. He continued his education in a local—but highly regarded—school of theology. His teacher, however, Clement of Alexandria, fled the city in the face of the persecution. Origen took the leadership of the school and began teaching in Clement's place. Still only a teenager, his brilliance attracted even more students. Demetrius, leader of the church in Alexandria, put him solely in charge of the teaching program, and unbelievers as well as Christians began to come to hear him. The curriculum was a mix of Christian theology and the thought of Plato. Clement had established this pattern to make Christian ideas understandable and palatable to the philosophically well-founded Alexandrians. Plato's idealism portrayed the world of matter as not quite real—not as real, in any case, as the spiritual realm—and Origen apparently bought into this view and maintained it through his lifetime.

Perhaps it was this otherworldly orientation that caused him to castrate himself while still very young. He taught women as well as men at his school, and maybe this rash action was in response to his awareness of sexual temptation. It does seem to be a rather too literal response to Jesus' comment about those "who have made themselves eunuchs for the kingdom" (Matthew 19:12). Origen's perception of the truth was over-spiritual, otherworldly, and he looked beyond physical reality and the plain meaning of the biblical text for the spiritual truths that were out of sight in the spirit world beyond. Perhaps he was encouraged in this direction by the gnosticism that flavored much of Christian thinking in Egypt. In any case, his orientation toward the spiritual ultimately moved him toward speculative theology—and heresy.

But in his quest for the truths of God he wrote much that remains beautiful today, and his personality was equally beautiful. How can we fault his zeal? He evangelized whomever he could. Though now viewed as a heretic, in his own time he confronted heretics and sometimes brought them to faith in Christ. One of those he won to Christ, Ambrose, was a wealthy Egyptian who had accepted the gnostic doctrines of Valentinus. In thanksgiving for Origen's teaching, Ambrose became his patron and financed Origen's writing career for the rest of his life.

Origen needed that support. His brilliance threatened the churchmen he came in contact with, especially Demetrius, now bishop of Alexandria. Although Origen wasn't yet ordained, his influential writings won him invitations to counsel the leaders of various churches in the East. He was asked to advise on matters of theological interpretation, and on one of these trips someone suggested that, rather than remain a layman preaching to bishops, he ought to undergo ordination. He agreed to this, but Demetrius was enraged, feeling the prerogative of his office had been undermined. Origen had made an enemy in his hometown.

While he had not fled the persecution of the world, this hostility from within the church became too much. He moved to Caesarea and continued teaching. New students came to study with him. He taught dialectics, physics, ethics, metaphysics, and theology. He was invited to Antioch to confer with the mother of the emperor. One of his greatest students was Gregory Thaumaturgos ("the wonderworker") who became a great evangelist in the area of Pontus (now Turkey). With eight secretaries paid by Ambrose, Origen continued to write nonstop and produced some six thousand works.

Toward the end of his life, another persecution of Christians, this one under the Emperor Decius, finally caught up with him. He was taken prisoner and tortured, was placed in a pillory, and had his legs stretched and twisted around a block—but he did not deny Christ. He probably would have welcomed martyrdom—and may have been treated differently by the later church had that come—but he survived the persecution and was freed. He was never the same, however, and about two years later, as he neared the age of seventy, he died.

For many years thereafter his teachings were highly regarded and extremely influential on the eastern church. Eusebius the Historian gave great attention to his life and writings. But as we'll see in the next chapter, a cataclysm of controversy was coming concerning the position of the Son of God in relation to the Father, and Eusebius (along with much of the eastern church) held an ambiguous view of Christ's divinity. The Arian controversy would resolve this, but in the process Origen's writings would be first demoted to less valuable status and then declared heresy and burned.

Origen believed that because the Son of God had been begotten by the Father, he was obviously less than the Father, as was the Holy Spirit. Tertullian's doctrine of the Trinity—which viewed Father, Son, and Holy Spirit as equal in divinity—had not completely taken hold in the East, and Origen's influence tilted the scale the other way.

Still, it's difficult to read Eusebius on Origen and not feel that Origen was trying his best to argue a nearly Trinitarian case. He debated Beryllus of Bostra, an Arabian bishop who believed that Christ did not preexist as an individual before he came among men and did not have any divinity of his own. Origen convinced Beryllus otherwise—toward what would seem to be a more Trinitarian position. Besides, as Origen argued in his *De Principiis*, while the apostles made themselves clear on many issues, there were other matters concerning which he said, "All this is not very clearly defined in the teachings." Still, it is certain that even in his own lifetime some of the leaders of churches around the Roman world had questions about his orthodoxy.

A clear definition of what the apostles actually taught in the New Testament was needed. Once that clarity came in the next century, Origen's writings, with their spiritual orientation and their tendency to interpret Scripture allegorically, seemed off the mark.

ORIGEN'S WRITINGS

Origen wrote a lot—apparently as fast as he could dictate. One of his greatest works we no longer have a copy of. It was called the *Hexapla*, and it was a parallel arrangement of the Hebrew Old Testament, the Greek translation of it called the Septuagint, and several other translations of the Old Testament that Origen had found. Another of his greatest works was *On First Principles*, or *De Principiis*, which reads like a primer in basic Christian beliefs.

Around the age of fifty he wrote *On Martyrdom*, in which he urged Christians to recognize the testimony inherent in martyrdom and to suffer martyrdom courageously. Certainly he must have run some of those lines over in his mind as his own legs were stretched on the blocks. Perhaps he gained some encouragement to be faithful to his own convictions. The record is that he was a strong encourager of others who went through these torments with him.

Perhaps his best known work is *Contra Celsum* or *Against Celsus*. Celsus had attacked Christianity in writing, and Origen responded to him in one of the earliest examples of apologetics.

ORIGEN'S CONTRIBUTIONS TO THE FAITH

Given the way the later church regarded Origen, it might be wondered if he made any positive contributions to the faith. However, he was clearly a student of the Scriptures and rarely made any statement without seeking a biblical foundation for his views. He believed in the inspiration and historicity of the Bible. He lived as an example of faithfulness and discipline. His words on prayer remain breathtakingly beautiful to this day, for with Origen—given his otherworldly nature—the person in prayer leaves this material universe to stand in the very presence of the Maker of heaven and earth.

He also was one of the first writers to make a clear distinction between the ideal church and the human church of principalities and politics. He spoke of a double church of men and of angels, the difference between the "lower church" and—in Platonist terms—the celestial ideal. Only the ideal church was the true church of Christ, scattered over all the earth. The earthly church provided a shelter for sinners.

ORIGEN'S MARGINAL SPECULATIONS

But those other, unorthodox statements of Origen attract most of our attention—they have the seeds of so many *different* heretical views. For one, Origen taught a three-level view of Scripture: He said that Scripture should be read for its surface, literal meaning, of course, and secondly for its moral application to the life of the reader. But the view he most preferred was the *allegorical* interpretation, in which persons, numbers, and so on symbolize something else. He speculated about the allegorical meanings of many Old Testament passages that otherwise seemed dry and barren of theological content, such as the Levitical laws.

For example, he said that Moses' injunction to acquire the Passover lamb on the tenth of the month but not to kill it until the fifteenth was an allegory of the five days that a candidate for baptism spent preparing to pass from a life of sin to a life of godliness. Each day related to a different one of the five senses. How did Moses know how this text would apply to Christians many years in the future? Divine inspiration caused him to intend a spiritual interpretation—absolutely in agreement with Origen's—for every one of Moses' laws. (Of course, I've heard a few preachers use worse allegories in modern sermons.)

While this approach to biblical interpretation might be shrugged off, Origen's belief that Christ was inferior to the Father would get him in trouble today. He said Christ was divine but laid aside his divinity when he became man. And while Origen argued that Christ existed before his conception in Mary's womb, he still said the Son was less than the Father.

Origen denied Jesus' bodily resurrection, seeing it instead as a spiritual body. That makes sense for Origen, given his orientation to the spiritual over the physical, but it's exactly at this point in history that the church as a whole was battling with the overly spiritual heresies of the gnostics. Origen wasn't helping.

We might also lay the theology of such movies as *It's a Wonderful Life* (where Clarence gets his wings) at Origen's feet, because he speculated that human souls could become angels or demons. This ties to what might be his wildest speculation — which will take a bit of explaining. He believed human souls exist before the baby's conception (this belief now shows up in Mormonism). He believed that our universe is only one of many sequential universes that God has made. We, as souls, have been moving through them and will continue to move through new creations until we *all* come to salvation. (Although he denied it, this sounds like a type of reincarnation, doesn't it?)

As to hell, Origen believed it had a *reformatory* purpose. Instead of eternal punishment, he saw it more like a place of purging (purgatory?) in preparation for moving on to another, higher spiritual level. In that sense, then, Origen was a universalist. He even held out hope that Satan himself would at last come to his senses and be saved—and that would then be the end. In all of this it is much easier to see Plato than Scripture in Origen's thought.

Yes, he was a heretic. But will this obvious lover of Christ Jesus, this firm believer in the Crucifixion and the (spiritual) resurrection, this battler for the truth of the Scriptures, this evangelist to those who did not believe, this near martyr who suffered horribly and yet would not deny his Lord, be present in heaven when we arrive there? How could we presume to make such judgments? I hope so. I'd like to spend some time talking with him personally, even if he did get rather speculative on some points.

People Like Us

Were Tertullian and Origen people like us? It's hard to conclude otherwise. They were fallible, imperfect—human. In some instances their humanness prevented them from making as much contribution to the kingdom of God as they might have. Tertullian's prickly personality distanced him from the church—whether by his choice or that of others or both, we really don't know. What might he have written with that scalpel-sharp wit if he'd not been consumed with his snarling judgments of others?

What might Origen have contributed if he had not become so enmeshed in the cerebral delights of philosophy? It's hard to imagine anybody writing more, but could his writings have been more practical, more down to earth, more—real? Let's just give thanks that—human though they were, and heretical at points—these two *people* shared with the world what they did.

The Body of Christ and the Human Institution

Clearly, both men saw the great gap between the ideal Christ established and what mankind had turned it into. Tertullian's struggles with the church authorities of his day made him reject the human institution entirely but not the Lord. There are Christians like him today: people who are so concerned about having a "pure" church that nobody except they themselves is pure enough to join. Origen never left the church, but he certainly had his share of trouble with church authorities. He wrote about the double church of men and of angels, and the way the lower church provided a haven for sinners. Both men saw need for reforms.

But *how* were such reforms to be made? By leaving the church, as Tertullian did? By leaving the basic truth of the gospel, as Origen did? Yes, institutions are flawed, often deeply flawed, as they are made up of people like us. But going to the other extreme of rejecting the institution of the church isn't a solution. Anti-institutionalists end up as lone rangers, certain that they alone are right and everybody else is mired in dead institutions. Going it alone leads to self-deception. God gave us the visible Christian community here on earth—the church—for a reason. It is not just an ideal church in some spiritual realm.

Faith Versus Reason

Both men made contributions to the tension between faith and reason. Tertullian scorned reason with his Jerusalem-Athens comment, yet he relied on it—the particular form he used being the dispute/debate logic of the legal system. Origen's form of rationality was the Platonic idealism that Tertullian blasted. We'd be more comfortable today with Tertullian's style than Origen's—it's more familiar to us as westerners. But both men affirmed the necessity of faith as the controlling factor in adjusting and taming reason. We may wish Origen had tamed his a little *more*, but his story shows how much the accepted style of thinking can change from generation to generation. In his day his understanding was widely appreciated. Three hundred years later, his books were burned. Yet his faith shines through in everything he wrote and did.

Church + State = Very Bad Things
At this point the church had not yet been married to the government.

What About Missions?
Missions had yet to be misplaced, for this was a missionary time when the faith was still struggling for a place of freedom in the empire.

Ethics Optional?
Was it already becoming the case that ethics appeared to be optional for Christians? Tertullian thought so and tried to do something about it through legalistic methods that didn't work. Origen didn't invest his energy in correcting the behaviors of others, but he certainly saw the problem. From the contributions of these two heretical fathers, it's difficult to define any approach that might help us deal with the problem today.

One last thing: Did you notice that both of these great minds came from Africa? The earliest church's leaders came from the Middle East (now Israel, Lebanon, Syria, and so on). Many from the next few generations came from Turkey and North Africa. Today we think of these as Muslim regions. So as we trace the history of Christianity's spread, pay attention to de-Christianization, too. Faith in Africa and the Middle East weakened between AD 400 and 600 to the point where Islam easily won and held those regions — not just by force, but because people didn't care enough about their Christian faith to defend it. In our century, the continent with the fastest growth in Christian faith is Africa, while Europe has drastically de-Christianized. It would be no surprise if the great Christian thinkers and leaders of the twenty-first century turned out to be Africans, Asians, or Latin Americans. And Europe? Its future hangs in the balance.

WANT TO KNOW MORE?

There are many valuable resources for learning more about Tertullian and Origen. Norman Geisler's *Baker Encyclopedia of Apologetics* (Grand Rapids, MI: Baker, 1998) has articles on both. Online, the Catholic Encyclopedia, www.newadvent .org/cathen/index.html, has excellent articles on both of these figures. So does Wikipedia (which isn't always reliable, but in this case is good). Joseph Wilson Trigg's *Origen* (Atlanta: John Knox Press, 1983) deals with Origen's life and theology in contrast with that of the more influential (on the West) Augustine.

By far the best resources on these two writers, however, are their own writings. There are many translations available. Check some out of the library and let these ancient believers speak to you directly. You'll not agree with everything they say, but you may find yourself understanding far better why they said it.

3

Fighting for Truth in the Imperial Church

CONSTANTINE AND ATHANASIUS

In the nineteen hundred or so years since the last living apostle died, who has most changed the church? A good argument could be made for Constantine. As the first "Christian" emperor, Constantine stopped the persecution of the church, forced the tolerance of Christians, and set in motion the process that led to the establishment of Christianity as the approved religion of the Roman Empire. He even presided over the Council of Nicea, which gave us the beginnings of the Nicene Creed and started to define the basics of Christian theology. Why did he become a Christian? Because he saw a cross in the sky.

FLAVIUS VALERIUS AURELIUS CONSTANTINUS
ca. 273–337

Born the son of the Roman general who was appointed as Caesar of the far Western Empire, Constantine was declared to be

"Augustus" by his father's army after his father died. In a series of battles and intrigues with and against the other Caesars, Constantine's power grew. Before the Battle of the Milvian Bridge outside Rome in AD 312, he had a vision of a cross in the sky and was told, "In this sign conquer." (The sign may, instead, have been the *chi rho* — the first two letters in the Greek spelling of *Christ*, which was already being used as a Christian symbol.) Interpreting it to mean he was to adopt the God of the Christians, Constantine put the sign on his soldiers' shields and won a great victory. Eventually he rose to become the sole emperor.

He made Christianity the approved religion of the empire, instituted Sunday as a special day on the calendar, and presided over the Council of Nicea, which he called to unify the church. He moved his capital from Rome to Constantinople (modern Istanbul, Turkey), thus *ensuring* the eventual division of the empire into East and West. He died soon after his baptism (which he delayed until shortly before his death to avoid any chance of sinning afterward). He was buried in a church he built for the twelve apostles, granting himself the title of "the Thirteenth Apostle."

IN THIS SIGN CONQUER

Eusebius described it this way:

> He said that about noon, when the day was already beginning to decline, he saw with his own eyes the trophy of a cross of light in the heavens, above the sun, and an inscription, CONQUER BY THIS attached to it. At this sight he himself was struck with amazement, and his whole army also, which followed him on an expedition and witnessed the

miracle. . . . Then in his sleep the Christ of God appeared to him with the sign which he had seen in the heavens, and commanded him to make a likeness of that sign . . . and to use it as a safeguard in all engagements with his enemies.[1]

Was Constantine telling the truth about what he saw? This story is somewhat different from the way he told it earlier to Lactantius, but Constantine often had trouble keeping his stories straight. In his climb to the ultimate spot in the Roman Empire, he tended to use whatever story best suited the situation, regardless of whether it was accurate or not. In that sense, perhaps the most certain thing we can say about Constantine the Great is that he was a consummate politician. This has caused some to question whether he ever actually became a Christian, or whether it was just the most politically expedient course to take at the time. Of course, we really can't judge that, can we? A person's relationship with God is between him or her and the Almighty, and we can't judge the state of another's heart.

We can, however, know many of the things Constantine said and did, and can interpret for ourselves whether his example was a good one to follow. We can also know this with clarity: Constantine was one of the most important figures in Christian history. When he came onto the stage, Christians were a persecuted minority. By the time he was baptized—on his deathbed—Christianity was the official religion of the Roman world, and the battle for what was to be called "orthodox" in the faith had begun in earnest.

Battle is probably a good metaphor for the 300s—political, martial, and theological. As Constantine won battles in the field, proving himself the best general of his time, Christians waged battle with one another over the proper interpretation of the gospel. We have another great figure of the faith, Athanasius, to thank for the understanding of the Trinity we hold today. These two greats helped shape us. It's only fitting that we know how they did it.

DIOCLETIAN SETS THE STAGE

We don't much like the concept of emperors today. We love our freedom. The idea of a single individual ruling with absolute power over everyone's life gives us chills (and makes for good fantasy and science fiction stories). But people in every generation want a strong leader when things are falling apart. In the mid 200s, Romans breathed a sigh of relief at the rise to absolute power of a tough general named Diocletian. You might think of him as being like Maximus from the film *The Gladiator*. He became emperor by stabbing his chief rival to death on the floor of the Roman Senate. (I guess it was easy to mop up blood off the marble—certainly enough of it was *shed* in that place over the centuries.) Diocletian has always been regarded as a devil by Christian sources. It was he, after all, who launched the last great persecution of the early church.

Why persecute Christians? One thing that infuriated the pagan upper classes of the empire was the way Christianity affected slaves and women. These were drawn to Christianity because the faith accorded them a level of value they didn't receive from the pagan system. Because much of the Roman bureaucracy was run by slaves and former slaves, Christians were gaining too much influence over the empire's daily operation. Influential Christians gave jobs to fellow Christians, partly out of friendship, but also because they could expect a level of honesty from fellow Christians that they couldn't necessarily count on from others. Eventually it became a good career move to convert to Christianity. That wasn't good for the long-term health of the church, as we will see. (On the other hand—don't some people still join a church today with mixed motives?) Diocletian saw this problem, and, being a practical sort, he moved to "correct" it.

But Diocletian was more than just a persecutor of Christians. He was also the emperor who restored the empire when it was about to come to pieces, and he set the stage for Constantine. He wisely recognized that such a vast territory as Rome had conquered couldn't be ruled effectively from one capital or by one man. He split his own rule with another, then set in motion a process of governmental succession that would prevent exactly the kind of coup that had brought him to power. He appointed a senior and a junior emperor for the Eastern Empire, where he settled, and another pair of emperors for the Western Empire. Then he retired. Maybe this was because most of the previous emperors had been murdered, and he wanted to die of old age. In any case, his plan didn't work. It *did*, however, lay the framework for Constantine to become emperor.

CONSTANTINE'S VICTORY

Constantine's father was one of the emperors Diocletian appointed for the far west. To secure his loyalty, Diocletian forced him to send Constantine to the court of Galerius, one of the emperors of the east. Under Diocletian and Galerius, Constantine proved a capable soldier. He must also have witnessed some terrible things, since of the four emperors Diocletian appointed, Galerius was the hardest on Christians. By contrast, Constantine's father (in present-day England) barely enforced the persecution of Christians at all.

Some have even suggested that Constantine's father was a Christian himself. (His name, confusingly, was Constantius Chlorus. So many of the members of Roman families had similar names that it seems clearer to describe them by relationship as much as possible.) His common-law wife, Constantine's mother, Helena, certainly *became* a Christian, but we don't exactly know when. And until the time Constantine saw the cross in the sky, his own faith seemed to be directed more to the sun god than to the Son of God.

The death of one of Diocletian's four appointed emperors required the appointment of a new "junior" Caesar, and most people expected it to be Constantine. Galerius, however, passed him over for another. Not long after that, Constantine's father asked that his son be returned to him in the British Isles because he was dying. Constantine was able to get away to England and helped his father in a battle against the Picts. His father died soon after, and on July 25, 306, the troops his father had commanded declared Constantine the new "Augustus."

This hardly resolved anything. There were, after all, three other active emperors and two in retirement who still fiddled in politics from time to time. Another was added when the son of one of these declared himself Caesar in Rome and took control of the capital. Constantine gradually dealt with these challenges to his rule in the West. He had the advantage of commanding an army of toughened veterans of the border wars with the barbarians of the north—and he was smart. A series of battles followed that resulted in Constantine advancing upon Rome, where his chief rival (of the moment, anyway) awaited.

At least, he *should* have waited. Instead, Maxentius marched out the gates of Rome to meet Constantine on the far side of the River Tiber, at the Milvian Bridge. This proved exceptionally stupid—so stupid that some writers of the time attributed his lapse in judgment to divine intervention. This was the first battle Constantine fought under the sign of the cross, and it was a total victory. On October 28, 312, Maxentius drowned as he tried to retreat across the river, and Constantine was the undisputed emperor of the Western Empire.

The eastern emperor, Licinius, was in the process of consolidating his own power, so he and Constantine met in Milan in 313 to make nice. Licinius married Constantine's half sister Constantia (see what I mean about the names?), and the two emperors agreed to grant religious tolerance to all groups, especially and particularly Christians. This is often called the Edict of Milan, and it actually was published by Licinius and not Constantine. For the first time, Christians were officially permitted to declare themselves publicly—or at least, that was the idea. In fact, Licinius began to persecute them again.

By 316 Licinius and Constantine were at war with one another. After an uneasy peace between 317 and 324 Constantine finally crushed Licinius, again with apparent help from the divine. A storm destroyed Licinius's battle fleet of 350 ships. In an act worthy of a Mafia don, Constantine spared Licinius's life at the pleading of his half sister—then later had him strangled. The whole empire now had a (ahem) "Christian" emperor.

CONSTANTINE'S CHRISTIAN MODEL?

How Christian was Constantine? It depends on who you read. The great Christian historian Eusebius of Caesarea—who knew Constantine and received support from him—

constantly flattered him in every way. Indeed, Constantine tended to flatter himself quite a bit. But in addition to killing Licinius after giving a solemn promise to spare him, he also had others murdered. Licinius's son — also named Licinius — he killed on suspicion that Licinius Jr. was plotting against him. He had his own first son, Crispus, killed because of some immoral act that Crispus reportedly committed — reported by Constantine's second wife, Fausta, who wanted Crispus out of the way to further the careers of her own three sons.

The reports of this event are contradictory. Did Crispus have an affair with Fausta? Did he try to rape her? Or did Fausta make all of it up? The Christian writers of the time didn't explain. It was all pretty sordid. But when Constantine's mother, Helena, scolded him for killing his own son, he had Fausta cooked to death in an overheated bath. Of course, Constantine felt positive that all of these actions were according to the will of God. He had a direct line to God, after all, and therefore was always right in his judgments. Let's face it: This kind of Christian is scary.

CONSTANTINE UNIFIES THE CHURCH — SORT OF

Constantine's spiritual self-certainty also applied to the church. He was certain that God wanted the church to be unified but was appalled to discover just how divided the church actually was. He discovered that the civil war within the church was just as sharp and the battle lines just as fiercely drawn as those in his own wars for imperial supremacy. He learned of the sharp contention between the Arians and the forces of Alexander and Athanasius concerning the relationship of Christ to God. He set out to resolve this problem, which will be our primary focus at the end of this chapter. He never succeeded in resolving it, although he did manage to introduce a nonbiblical Greek word into the debate as the *decisive* word. We'll soon see what this word was and how the debate turned out.

CONSTANTINOPLE

Besides reunifying the empire and recognizing the church, Constantine also moved the capital to the old Greek city of Byzantium. This city was on the Bosphorus, the strait that joins the Black Sea with the Sea of Marmara and the Aegean Sea and that separates Europe from Asia. Byzantium (renamed Constantinople) quickly became Rome's rival in beauty, power, and population—and almost assured the eventual permanent division of the empire between the two cities. For a millennium, Constantinople stood astride two continents and influenced events until it was finally conquered by the Muslim Turks and renamed Istanbul.

Why Constantinople? It was here that Constantine had finally defeated Licinius, so he knew the strategic value of the location. Also, while in the West only one person in five was a Christian, in the Eastern Empire almost half the population was Christian. Here Constantine made his home, founded churches, and intervened in church affairs for good or ill. He had no conception of the value of separation of the church from the state. As a result, he used the church as an instrument of imperial policy and forced upon it his own ideology, removing from it the independence it had enjoyed as a persecuted minority.

We have plenty of ammunition to debate Constantine's character as an emperor and as a Christian. We may question whether he was a hero of the church or more a spoiler of its purity and evangelistic fervor. But there was a true hero of the faith at this time who made more of a difference to the faith we know today than even the emperor. Athanasius of Alexandria took seriously the verse in Jude that says, "Contend earnestly for the faith which was once for all delivered to the saints" (verse 3). He fought all his life to maintain the divinity of Christ. Our understanding of the Trinity rests largely on the understanding of Athanasius—and on his intrepid defense of his view in the face of those who didn't believe Christ was equal with God.

IS CHRIST DIVINE?

Think about this for a moment: What if Christ Jesus weren't the divine Word? What if Jesus was—as many gnostic sects claimed—only God's representative, a created being? The Muslims are comfortable with this. They believe Jesus was the great prophet *Isa*, second only to Muhammad in revealed truth, but certainly not divine. Those today who say Jesus was just a great man and a wonderful teacher would apparently feel good about this idea. This view makes it much easier to fit Christianity in with the other world religions, to say, "All religions point to the same God."

That would make Christianity a philosophy for living one's life, but not *the* way, *the* truth, and *the* life of salvation. It would make the cross a tragic consequence of the politics of first-century Judea, nothing more. If Christ Jesus is not the incarnation of God on earth, why would his death have any effect on our sins? He would just be another guy who tried to change the world—and eventually succeeded, in a way, but got killed doing it. If this is the case, how could he be our Savior? What difference would the death of a Judean philosopher of two thousand years ago make to our immortal souls? And since we've mentioned it, if Jesus was just a man and the cross only a tragedy, why would we need to hold to that hard-to-explain doctrine of the Resurrection?

The idea that Christ was not divine was not new. The particular form of it that Athanasius battled was taught in his time by a man named Arius and so came to be called Arianism. As the young assistant to Alexander, bishop of Alexandria, at the Council of Nicea, Athanasius took his stand on the divinity of Christ and made it clear that any other view was heresy. The fact that Emperor Constantine tolerated Arian views and that for the rest of Athanasius's life the imperial court in Constantinople was swayed by its adherents did not alter Athanasius's convictions. This is why he is still known today as the "Father of Orthodoxy."

ATHANASIUS'S EARLY LIFE

Athanasius grew up in that great educational center of Alexandria in Egypt, where Apollos, Clement, and Origen all got their training. We've seen that these men tried to adapt the Christian message to the Platonic mind-set of their times — to make the gospel reasonable for Greco-Roman culture. Athanasius was apparently raised in this same tradition.

ATHANASIUS
ca. 297–373

Born and educated in the Egyptian city of Alexandria, Athanasius became the chief defender of orthodoxy against the Arian heresy that the Son was subordinate to the Father. Alexander, bishop of Alexandria, made Athanasius his student early on, and

Athanasius was a clear-thinking, outspoken young man when the battle with Arian thinking was joined at the Council of Nicea in 325. He became bishop of Alexandria when his mentor died, then embarked upon years of continued struggle with the politically well-placed Arians. He was banished from Alexandria five times but returned to jubilant crowds each time. He could be a tough infighter, and he was not opposed to using violence if he thought it would advance the cause of salvation.

The date of his birth is disputed but seems to have been around 297. Legends suggest he came from a wealthy family and therefore had the benefit of a formal education. Others say that Bishop Alexander saw promise in him when he was still a boy. In fact there's a story that after a major Christian celebration Alexander looked out the window of his study and saw a group of boys playing church down by the ocean. One of the boys was pretending to be the bishop, baptizing the others. Alexander wanted to meet him. This was Athanasius, and Bishop Alexander was impressed. The bishop decided to recognize the baptisms of those Athanasius had baptized and began to teach the boy himself. Like other colorful stories surrounding the people of this time, this may be more legend than fact. But however it happened, Athanasius came early both to faith in Christ and leadership in the church.

A later emperor, Julian (known as "the Apostate" for trying to turn the empire away from Christianity and back to pagan religions), contemptuously described Athanasius as a little man. He was apparently short, wiry, and energetic, with fiery eyes, a quick wit, and intuition to grasp ideas and their implications quickly. His sense of humor could be cutting to those he opposed, and while he could be pleasant in conversation, he apparently never let up when he was in debate. He had great courage in his convictions, even when it appeared his cause was losing. While his classical education served him well, he gave his life to defending the integrity of the faith. His surrender to Christ was genuine and all-consuming. Taken as a whole, Athanasius was a short man with a big mind and an even bigger will—which he did his best to commit wholly to Christ Jesus.

THE RISE OF ARIUS

As Constantine conquered his empire and Athanasius studied to become a priest, a presbyter (lower than priestly rank) named Arius taught that Christ couldn't be equal to God because there was a time when he hadn't existed and was therefore a creature *made* by God.

There had long been a strong gnostic streak in Egypt, which is where Alexander, Athanasius, and Arius all came from. The gnostic gospel of Thomas and gospel of Judas both had their main fans in Egypt. Many people there must have been inclined to question Christ's divinity, for Arianism spread quickly in the Eastern Empire.

Arius accused Bishop Alexander of the heresy of Sabellianism—the tendency to regard the Father, Son, and Holy Spirit as different "modes" or guises of God. (This, by the way, is the reason why that old standard explanation that uses water, ice, and steam to describe the Trinity is actually heretical.) In response, Alexander excommunicated Arius for heresy. The Christian world—in the Eastern Empire, at least—was sharply divided. The new Emperor Constantine called for a council in Nicea to settle the issue and reunite the church.

Reunite might be the wrong word. Was it ever truly united? There had long been diverse viewpoints among the churches scattered across the empire. There continued to be debates about which of the circulating Scriptures were actually true and worthy, and which were not. There were differences of opinion as to when to celebrate various holy days. There were sharp disagreements about whether to allow Christians who had offered sacrificial incense to Emperor Diocletian (to avoid martyrdom) back into the fellowship with those who had risked their lives by refusing. The Roman Empire was a diverse conglomeration of peoples and cultures united by one thing: the power of the Roman legions.

This was, in fact, one of the primary reasons why the authorities persecuted the church for so long: Christians showed loyalty to their God instead of to the imperial idea. They'd proved themselves willing to die for their differing beliefs rather than join with the rest of the conquered peoples in pledging allegiance to the emperor as a god. (By contrast, the pagan Roman government never had a problem with the gnostics and never persecuted them, because gnostics didn't mind participating in worship of the emperor and other imperial gods. It wasn't until Christianity became the empire's official religion that gnostics began to face persecution.)

Thus, given that willingness to die for the faith was a core Christian attitude in this period, it's not surprising that Christians were willing to confront one another in the strongest terms when they disagreed over the faith.

THE COUNCIL OF NICEA

Constantine regarded these disagreements as insignificant. Obviously, he hadn't spent much time attending church business meetings. He paid the travel expenses for leaders willing to come to Nicea in 325 to debate the questions, but because it was in the east a preponderance of eastern clergy attended. Only six attendees came from the west. The meeting produced the first version of what is known today as the Nicene Creed, and the big point at issue was the relationship of God the Father to Christ Jesus—in other words, Arianism.

On the counsel of his advisers, Constantine suggested that the Greek word *homoousion* be inserted into the creed to explain this relationship. It meant that Christ is identical in substance to the Father, coessential or consubstantial with him. It's not a term found in the Bible. It's a philosophical term. But it became the heart of the new creed, and at the insistence of the emperor, the council accepted it. Constantine thought this settled things. He was wrong.

BISHOP OF ALEXANDRIA

Athanasius didn't like the word much himself. He didn't use it much in his writings. But as Alexander's secretary and confidant, he endorsed it, since it did establish to some degree the principle of the unity of the Godhead. His performance at Nicea marked him as a chief opponent of the Arians, and when Alexander died five months after the council, Athanasius—still under thirty years old—was made the new bishop of Alexandria.

Consider for a moment how long it had been since the Resurrection events in Jerusalem: almost three hundred years. Do the events of the early 1700s seem like yesterday to you? Or like ancient history? It must have seemed a long, long time to Athanasius and his contemporaries since the time of Jesus, Peter, John, and Paul. The church had become an empire-wide organization with assets and influence and—now that there was a Christian emperor—political power. The young bishop became the lightning rod for Arian political attacks. He was accused of a laundry list of charges, and since many of the Christian leaders around Constantinople had Arian leanings, Constantine got an earful of them.

The charges would have been less effective if there hadn't been some truth in them. Athanasius wasn't above using violence to accomplish God's purposes. In a time when theological issues were sometimes resolved by street fighting, he apparently had gangs of thugs at his disposal that could go into the alleyways and battle for the truth. When Constantine was trying to get the entire church to accept diverse views—the "can't we all just get along" approach—Athanasius was unflinchingly restrictive. When Constantine wrote to him directly requesting that those condemned priests who were ready to submit to the new creed should be readmitted to the priesthood, Athanasius said no. There could be no fellowship between the true church and those who denied Christ's divinity.

Tired of being thwarted by a young preacher, Constantine ordered Athanasius to be tried by a synod of Christian leaders at Tyre. When it became apparent that he would not receive a fair hearing there, Athanasius decided to appeal directly to the emperor. One day as Constantine was returning from a hunt, Athanasius stepped out in front of him and demanded a fair hearing before his accusers. Constantine was shocked, but he agreed and summoned the leaders from Tyre (who had condemned Athanasius in his absence). Athanasius lost his case, and Constantine banished him about as far away in the empire as he could go—to Treves, the imperial capital on the northwestern border with the German barbarians.

There, Constantine's son (named, of course, Constantine) was in charge. Constantine Jr. welcomed Athanasius, and he remained there about two and a half years. During his exile he taught monasticism to the churches in Europe—things he had learned from the great Saint Anthony of the Egyptian desert.

While Athanasius was gone, Arius was found dead in a public toilet in Constantinople. Athanasius saw this as the judgment of an angry God. A year later, on May 22, 337, Constantine Sr. died.

DEATH OF CONSTANTINE

He'd been preparing for a new war with Persia when he became ill. He'd wanted to be baptized in the Jordan River, but he was also planning to wait until he was on his deathbed to take this last formal step into the Christian faith. Knowing his end was near, Constantine put off his royal robes and put on the white baptismal robes of a new Christian and was baptized. He never took them off.

He had built in Constantinople the Church of the Twelve Apostles, and he was buried there, assuming one last title: the Thirteenth Apostle. He had changed the course of the church—but was the new course all that good? He had introduced imperial politics into the church, and if you wonder whether it's a good idea for the church to marry the state, you be the judge as you keep reading.

In any case, Athanasius's exile turned out to benefit him because Constantine Jr. was now emperor, and he and Athanasius were friends. When he came to the throne, he invited his friend to resume his place as bishop of Alexandria. Athanasius was back, and the people cheered! Of course, he was to be banished again. And again. Five times through the course of his life he was banished, for the Arian party was politically well-positioned, and Constantine's other sons — Constantius and Constans — eventually ruled parts of the empire. (Constans was Arian.)

The history of the succeeding years is intricate and confusing. None of the next several emperors lived long, and as the throne changed hands, so too did power in the church. Athanasius came in and out and in and out of favor, but he took it all bravely and finished his life defending Christ's divinity and the apostolic faith. He also urged that the Holy Spirit be seen as part of the Godhead, helping to ensure the Trinitarian formula that Christians hold today. Does that make him a true hero of the faith?

Some historians say no, citing his willingness to use beatings, intimidation, kidnapping, and imprisonment to silence those who opposed him. These don't sound like the practices of the pious believer, but Athanasius justified them by saying that the argument with Arianism was not just over a theological theory but was a threat to salvation.

People Like Us

Clearly, both Constantine and Athanasius were people like us — sinners with histories and failings who nevertheless thought they were doing God's will. They both had lots of friends, but they also had many enemies — enemies willing to say and write the worst about them. Should we make them our models? There are principles they each fought for that ought to be part of our beliefs and others that shouldn't be. You need to decide for yourself how their stories should affect yours.

The Body of Christ and the Human Institution

What about the church during this period of history? How much of it was the body of Christ and how much a human institution? Think about the context. For three hundred years, Christians had been discriminated against, hunted, and killed for their beliefs. They had the stories (and the bones) of martyrs who had suffered through this terrible injustice. It's no wonder they leaped at the chance to help change the political landscape at the invitation of the new emperor. But maybe the comfort of political approval is not a blessing to the faith, but a virus. It didn't take long before the institution of Roman government became the skeleton of the church, and the body of Christ did some bad things.

Faith Versus Reason

Given Constantine's non-Christian understanding of religion, it's easy to understand why he thought it reasonable to institutionalize Christianity and make it the favored religion in the empire. Roman households customarily followed the religion of the family patriarch, so if Constantine was the head of the imperial family, he got to pick its religion, didn't he? If he thought it was the most reasonable faith, shouldn't everybody else agree? The unity of the church also seemed to him a reasonable goal, and he felt understandably frustrated that Christian leaders failed to get with his program. He wanted to unify his empire politically by unifying it religiously. Those who apparently wanted to divide it—like Athanasius—became what emperors had often seen Christians to be: disloyal to the imperial idea.

The battle between orthodoxy and Arianism too was waged in terms of reason versus faith. The orthodox view of the

Scriptures and the apostles was that Jesus was divine. It was reason flavored by Greek philosophy and gnostic ideas that called Christ's divinity into question. To the Greek way of thinking, it seemed philosophically logical that Christ couldn't be equal to the Father. Monotheism means one god. How could anybody add Father plus the Son plus the Holy Spirit and still have one God? It was confusing—it still is, especially to Muslims, who call Trinitarian Christians polytheists.

Arius used logic to argue that if the Son came from the Father, then the Father created him. In the Greek portion of the empire that logic made sense. Athanasius, however, argued from Scripture, which defies logic by presenting God as both Three and One at the same time. It took more than a century before this view, which we call orthodoxy, carried the day.

Church + State = Very Bad Things/What About Missions?

When the church married the state, one immediate effect was that it interrupted missions. There had been a growing church in Persia, but after Christianity became the official religion of the Roman Empire, the Persians began to view Christians as Roman infiltrators. In northwestern Europe, too, tribes viewed Christian conversion as the same as submission to Rome. And they didn't want that.

Constantine felt good about his own missionary efforts—he required tribes that he conquered along the Danube to convert—but should we applaud forced conversions? Later emperors felt no such need to evangelize, and church leaders, having risen to political preeminence, often spent far more of their time jostling for political status than spreading the good news. It was left for the church in the far western British

Isles to take up the cause of missions and truly evangelize the European tribes, which it did with great success in succeeding centuries. Tribes forced by their leaders to become Christian in name gradually became more Christian in understanding and action as well.

Another problem with church + state was that once Christianity became *the* religion to have, politicians became Christians to advance their careers. Even today political figures embrace the church to gain votes. We don't want to judge others' faith, but imagine if all the politicians who claimed to be Christian actually voted in a Christlike way. Do we have Constantine to thank for political hypocrisy in succeeding generations?

Further, in its forced marriage with the state, the church lost much of its independence. The emperor started fixing theology. The church gained political influence but lost much of its evangelical and moral influence. It lost important parts of its identity as Christ's body on earth.

It's good for us to remember, however, that the Holy Spirit can't be checkmated by human actions. Throughout church history, there have always been those who have maintained their influence and identity as Christ's body, who have acted as Christ's hands and feet, ears, eyes, and mouth.

Ethics Optional?

Was it ethical for Constantine to break his promises and kill those whose lives he'd sworn to spare? Was it ethical for him to spill blood from the west to the east under the sign of the cross? Was it ethical for him to quietly assassinate enemies, strangers, and even family members in the pursuit of his ambitions? Perhaps we shouldn't hold him to too high a standard.

After all, he was a Roman emperor. But what about the bishop of Alexandria? Was it ethical for Athanasius to use violence to subdue his enemies for the cause of Christ? Did his hard-nosed tactics cause his many banishments, depriving his people of the Christian leader they knew and loved? Actions have consequences. Are ethics optional? We'll meet this question again and again as we trace the church's history. But somehow this question rolls us back around to the first of our themes—the sinful nature of mankind. We all are sinners saved by grace.

No one outside of the New Testament made that point more forcefully than the next saint we'll study: Augustine of Hippo.

WANT TO KNOW MORE?

Constantine was one of the central figures of secular history as well as church history. There are many resources available to learn more about him. An excellent biography is Michael Grant's *Constantine the Great: The Man and His Times* (New York: Scribner's, 1994), which provides background for this whole period. You might look up Constantine and Athanasius on Wikipedia, remembering that these articles are only as acurate as the contributor who wrote them, but these articles also have extensive bibliographies that will give you new sources to follow. The Catholic Encyclopedia (also online) incorporates well-researched articles on these figures too.

4

Confession Is Good for the Church

AUGUSTINE

I must confess I grew tired of my father's preaching. Literally, sometimes: His voice would put me to sleep, there in the back row. What really woke me up were the guest speakers he regularly scheduled—people with *stories*. Sometimes those stories tiptoed along the edge of the sordid, tales of alcohol and drugs and promiscuity, leading up to the realization of the need for repentance and salvation. These weren't sermons—in my church tradition they were called *testimonies*. And since I knew all about the salvation part, but had been pretty sheltered from any descriptions of sin, these details of the forbidden fruit seemed particularly juicy.

I knew early on that I, too, would be a preacher, but I can remember *consciously* deciding that I needed to "get a good testimony" first. You know, to hold the kids' attention once I'd changed.

Well, I did. But that's not the focus of this chapter. Instead, let's look at the man who set the pattern for public confessions and went on to lay the foundation of Western Christian theology. Despite the prayers and pleas of his godly mother, Augustine dove headlong into the vat of sin and got himself good and filthy before he accepted the truth. Once he did, he set about trying to scrub clean what he'd made so dirty, and he ran headlong into an understanding of God's grace. Augustine's experience of that grace, and his willingness to share it, made a difference in the church of his time. It continues to make a difference today.

(AURELIUS AUGUSTINUS)
354–430

Born in North Africa not far from Carthage, Augustine was raised by his mother to be a Christian but wasn't baptized. Instead, he followed the heretical sect called Manichaeism and (by his own account) his own lusts. A brilliant student of rhetoric, he became a teacher and eventually found his way to Rome. While there he suffered a crisis in his beliefs and experienced a life-transforming encounter with Christ Jesus. He became as committed to the orthodox Christian faith as he had once been opposed to it. He was made bishop of Hippo in North Africa and served in that capacity for most of his life. Through his writings he came to be regarded as the greatest theologian of the faith after Paul. His *Confessions* and *The City of God* are numbered among the great books of Western thought. Roman Catholics, Anglicans, and Eastern Orthodox Christians regard him as a saint. Protestants — especially Calvinists — see him as the foundational theologian of the Reformation because of his teachings on grace and salvation.

AUGUSTINE'S LIFE

Most Christian scholars agree that Paul was the greatest of Christian theologians. But if there is a primary choice for the *second* most important theologian — at least for the Western church — it's Augustine. By the time he died, he was the leading bishop of a church at Hippo (yup, funny name) in North Africa, and was highly regarded by the entire Christian world. But like the other people we have dealt with in this book, Augustine was just a person. He wasn't always a great spiritual leader and writer. In fact, much like Paul, Augustine considered himself to be a great sinner. He surely made a good case for that being true.

He was born in a small town in North Africa, which was largely Christianized in the fourth century and very much a part of the Roman world. Carthage had been Rome's chief rival in the early days of the Roman republic, and the two had fought the Punic wars almost continually until Rome finally won. The Romans had then occupied North Africa all the way south to the edge of the Sahara, and in Augustine's time Rome was the great city, the goal of the young and ambitious. Like New York today, if you could make it there, you could make it anywhere. As a teen Augustine got that goal into his sights, and he ultimately achieved it. On the way, he sacrificed his morals and his moorings. It's not a new story, really.

His father was a pagan, but Augustine was blessed by a gift that so many of the greats of the church possessed: a godly and relentless mother. Monica raised him in the Christian faith, but babies weren't baptized in those days and Augustine avoided signing up when he was old enough to choose. He got sick as a boy and nearly got baptized then, but when the illness passed so did his reason to believe. And he had already found his real love: literature. The writings of Virgil and the orations of Cicero captured him. Along with these came a skeptical viewpoint that caused him to regard the Bible with something near contempt.

He had a lightning-fast mind. Many of those who study human intelligence regard it in terms of speed—almost anyone can learn almost anything, given enough time. But like a blazing-fast new computer that can think rings around an old machine with a lesser chip and little RAM, Augustine's mind ran laps around the minds of the boys around him. He could learn anything almost immediately—except Greek. For some reason, he found that language tedious and never really learned it. (I can think of hundreds of seminary students who share Augustine's frustration on this point.) Everything else he could learn he scooped into his mind, quickly catching up to and passing his teachers.

His parents decided he needed to study in Carthage. But at the age of sixteen, while waiting to start his education in Carthage, he discovered what would be his life's greatest hindrance: lust. Augustine loved love, but he didn't love people. Instead he loved the feelings associated with sex. He began an affair with a girl whose name we don't even know—even though we know more about Augustine than any of the other early church fathers. He never married her (she was beneath his social station, and he was holding out for a high-class wife), but they slept together for fifteen years and had a child.

From his Christian upbringing, Augustine knew there was a problem here. He came to believe sexuality was inherently dirty, but he couldn't prevent himself from pursuing it. This same attitude toward sexuality has plagued the church into the present, and Augustine's eloquent writing both about his experience and his view of sex has helped to foster a cringing prudishness toward one of God's most precious gifts.

WITH THE MANICHAEANS

Augustine's desires compelled him into promiscuity, but his spirit wouldn't let him pursue that course without feeling troubled. He began to follow the teaching of the Manichaeans, a cult that claimed to be Christian but that he later called "a great decoy of the devil." The Manichaeans emphasized winning one's own salvation through good works. The cult was a recent import from Persia that was sweeping through the Roman world. But its ideas weren't new — in chapter 1 we talked about gnosticism, that distinction between the material world and the "spiritual" reality that saw matter as bad and spirit as good.

The founder of Manichaeism, Mani, claimed to be the voice of the Holy Spirit. (That's pretty much a tip-off of a cultic organization, even today.) This was a two-class religion: There were the elect, who remained holy and pure and lived above the world, with the expectation that this would be their last life, and there were the laypeople, who brought the elect food and followed Mani's teachings. These laypeople expected to be reincarnated to get another chance to make life right. This second category provided Augustine with the opportunity to continue his "love" life while pretending to be religious. It went along with what he said he prayed: "Lord, give me chastity. Just not *now*!"

This chance to have his cake and eat it too was apparently enough to keep the sharp-minded young skeptic from questioning some odd beliefs. While the Manichaeans claimed to offer pure reason in place of faith, they really didn't provide good *reasons* to believe what they did. However, it took a long time for Augustine to come to that realization. Instead he bought Mani's version of what is called *dualism*. Dualists believe there are two equally powerful forces at war in the universe. Good and evil are equally powerful and continually contend with one another. Mani said five elements fought a constant war with the five dens of darkness. (Are we seeing some of these myths recycled in modern cartoons like *Avatar: The Last Airbender*?) The main problem with dualism is that it overvalues evil's power and undervalues God's power. A number of horror writers and movies today seem to do this. They represent Satan as God's equal—or almost so. According to Scripture, it's not even a contest. God has already won.

In some ways, the Manichaeans were the mental descendents of the Marcionites, for they hated and rejected the Old Testament God while they believed the New Testament was corrupted. Augustine was taught that the Old Testament God was barbaric. This helped him to reject the Bible, along with his mother's teaching. And while the elect practiced celibacy, there was no requirement for the layman to do so. Not surprisingly, Augustine remained a layman.

Though he was doing great in school, his mother loathed his new religion. Still she continued to pray for him, trying to find one bishop or another who would go and talk to her son about his beliefs. One pastor, watching her weep, told her not to worry, saying, "It is impossible that the son of these tears should perish." Monica kept praying.

TRANSFORMATION

After graduating from Carthage, Augustine became a schoolmaster, but by age twenty-six he was fed up with his rowdy students and went to Rome. He'd won a prestigious poetry contest and had great hopes. His wealthy patron, Romanianus, agreed to finance his travel to the great city. Several of his friends, as well as his girlfriend and son, traveled to Rome with him. Monica didn't want him to go and followed him all the way to the sea, pleading with him. He slipped away in the night.

But Rome wasn't particularly kind to this ambitious young man from the sticks of Africa. Students there were even rowdier than in Carthage, so he moved to Milan. There he met the great Bishop Ambrose, a wonderful preacher. As a student of oratory, Augustine went to hear Ambrose speak and eventually began to pay attention to the content as well as the style. Ambrose motivated Augustine to reexamine his understanding of the Bible and even to *read* it.

His encounter with the Scriptures—particularly the writings of Paul—helped him see that salvation doesn't come by our good works (especially since none of us can do any good works without God!). Instead, he learned, salvation comes through the grace (gift) of God's forgiveness through Christ's death for our sins. Augustine had already put his Manichaeism aside, but he'd found nothing to replace it. He was in his garden weeping when he heard a child in the neighborhood singing, "Take and read, take and read." He took this as a personal message and picked up Paul's writings and read. His eyes fell on Romans 13:13-14: "Let us walk properly, as in the day, not in revelry and drunkenness, not in lewdness and lust, not in strife and envy. But put on the Lord Jesus Christ, and make no provision for the flesh, to fulfill its lusts." These words struck straight to his heart—and to the sin that had long degraded him.

> You stir man to take pleasure in praising you, because you have made us for yourself, and our heart is restless until it rests in you.
>
> AUGUSTINE, *CONFESSIONS*

Augustine's life turned around. His mother had followed him to Rome and was keeping house for him. She rejoiced to see her prayers answered. He broke off his sinful activity, but he didn't marry his girlfriend. Instead, he took a vow of celibacy. His society considered it perfectly okay for him to send his lower-class mistress back to Africa and keep their teenage son with him. She never saw her son again, and we don't know what happened to her. (Conversion to Christ didn't automatically wipe out Augustine's blind spots, especially where women were concerned.)

He won his friends — those whom he had converted to Manichaeism — to Christ. Ambrose baptized them all. Augustine formed a sort of study group — really a monastic order without the title. Then Monica became ill, and Augustine and his brother tried to get her home to die in Africa. She wasn't worried about where she would be buried, saying that on the last day the Lord would find her wherever she was. They buried her in Italy, then went back to North Africa.

AFRICA AND ORDINATION

Augustine devoted the rest of his life to preaching and writing about God's grace. He quit teaching school and began writing. In his *Confessions*, he told his own story in depth and with great honesty and repentance. He established a monastery in his hometown of Tagaste and would have been happy to spend his life in study and conversation, but his gifts were too great to go unrecognized. On a visit to the large city of Hippo on the North African coast, he was praying in a chapel when he was surrounded by a large group of admirers. The current bishop of Hippo was aged and wanted to train a successor, and the people wanted Augustine. He pleaded with them not to put this burden on him, begging them with tears to let him return to his contemplative life, but at last he relented and was ordained to the priesthood. He became associate bishop for about five years, then, at age forty-two, assumed the full responsibility. For the next thirty-four years he served in this position of great responsibility and influence. He preached regularly—sometimes five days in a row—and wrote in response to the problems of the time.

AGAINST THE MANICHAEANS

He felt the need to counter the influence of the sect he had once belonged to. He wrote books refuting the teachings of Mani and other Manichaean leaders. When Felix, a highly respected Manichaean leader (and one of the elect), came to spread his teachings in Hippo, Augustine engaged him in a great debate. He was, of course, perfectly prepared for this encounter: He knew the Manichaean doctrine thoroughly and could spell out the problems with it he had discovered through his long experience.

The Manichaeans argued that they could show the way to God through reason. Augustine knew better and made that clear. He voiced his principle, "Believe in order to understand," which has caused him to be associated with those throughout Christian history who have favored faith over reason. Of course, he used reason to explain his principle—so well that he not only won the debate but won Felix to Christianity.

Augustine continued to use his influence to gradually elim-inate the sect throughout North Africa. Interesting, isn't it, how God used Augustine's early failures to bring about the end of a heretical sect? There's that value of "having a testimony." (Please hear me being facetious here! The consequences are certainly not worth it!)

AGAINST THE DONATISTS

His next great battle involved a problem that had racked the church of North Africa since the time of Tertullian. This might be called the legalist movement. Remember that Tertullian had been concerned about holiness to the point of eventu-ally starting his own extremely narrow sect. Beginning in the Montanist movement and continuing through the Novationist and Donatist movements (these names came from the names of various leaders in different times), those holding these beliefs insisted that Christians must live in sinless perfection after baptism. Each of these groups wanted to deny sinners' continued relationship to the body of Christ. The fallen must be put out of the church and could not be restored. Most of the Catholic pastors, now called bishops, took a much more forgiving position toward the fallen, finding ways of reopening the church to those who had failed.

In Augustine's time it was the Donatists who maintained this "high" view of holiness, and they shunned the larger body of the Catholic Church. The particular form of the problem by this time had to do with the worthiness of restored priests to continue in service. The Donatists argued that sacraments administered by such fallen sinners would be worthless.

Augustine tried to be a go-between to help restore the

Donatists to the fold—but they would have none of it. In their self-righteousness they'd begun to do violence to those who disagreed with them, forcing succeeding emperors to take police action against them. It appears that the North African Donatist movement may have had a political element—that those who wanted to be free of Roman rule found expression for their views through the schism (that means split or break) from the church.

At first Augustine opposed military action against the Donatists, trying instead to build relationships and sending representatives to reason with them. But when several of his friends were beaten by Donatist fanatics—and after he'd weathered a couple of attempts to assassinate him—he decided that strict laws against Donatist violence were in order. When this meeting of strength with strength resulted in many conversions of Donatists back into the church, Augustine felt confirmed in his views. He never, however, came to the place that he believed these heretics should be *killed* for their beliefs.

In the debate with the Donatists Augustine developed the doctrine that the church could always include sinners in the fold for the purpose of converting them. His views also helped to justify the church's right to use political power to assert spiritual control. Did this strengthen the ties between the church and the state? Probably. Augustine's theological position conferred on the church alone the power to provide or withhold the sacraments, thus giving the church control of salvation.

The stresses of office and the continuing battles had made him more pessimistic. He was developing a view of history and human nature that drew a sharp line between the kingdoms of this world and the kingdom of God. He was to write about this extensively in what many believe to be his greatest work, *The City of God*.

THE CRUMBLING EMPIRE

The Roman Empire was in a long downward slide. When Constantine moved his capital to Constantinople, the western half of the empire (still ruled by Rome) was already in danger from the attacking tribes of the north. These Germanic tribes were Arians. They didn't believe in Christ's divinity or the Trinity. What they mostly believed in was conquering land, and they did so, creeping closer and closer to Rome. When the Goths sacked Rome in 410, people of the West thought the world was coming apart. Some pagan writers blamed Rome's fall on Christians.

The City of God is subtitled *Against the Pagans*. It's hard for us to read today because it's loaded with historical specifics that are meaningless to all but classical historians. It's a Christian historical philosophy of civilization, full of Augustine's insights into — well, almost everything. But his general point is clear: The "city of man" represents all the cultures and institutions that have passed through history and disappeared. Culture is of no final value if God so wills. The lasting city is the heavenly city of God, led and inspired by the church. From the moment of the church's birth, the struggle between good and evil has been intense. Human salvation rests on the church as the earthly embodiment of the city of God.

But — and this is important — the separation between the city of man and the city of God isn't cut-and-dried. Augustine said the state isn't merely earthly and wicked; its role is to preserve the church. Likewise, the church isn't perfect. God could withdraw his mandate from the church, just as he withdrew it from Israel during the Babylonian captivity. The removal of this blessing—resulting in repentance and revival among God's people—could explain why God allowed the sack of Rome.

That's how Augustine saw it, and his interpretation of history continues to affect the world—and the church—to this day.

INVASION OF THE PELAGIANS

The sack of Rome affected North Africa in more practical ways too. First, while Rome was looted, it didn't disappear. It continued on, largely unchanged, and recovered enough to be worth sacking again in 455. Still, many refugees fled Rome and Italy, and among those who fled to North Africa were Pelagius and Celestius. Pelagius had attacked the doctrine of original sin, the concept that because Adam and Eve fell, all of their children are born already sinners and in need of salvation. Pelagius preferred the idea that each individual might be punished for his or her *own* sin, but that each individual is created without corruption. It might be possible that a person could live so righteously that he or she would never need salvation. We have free will, he argued. Sin is the deliberate choice of evil.

Think how Augustine must have heard this. Having chosen early a depraved life that had in it no hope of salvation, Augustine had been transformed by God's grace—grace that was greater than his sin. He had responded to this grace through faith, and his understanding of that grace had grown through his faith. Despite intense effort, he had found it impossible to resist sin without grace, and he was convinced it was impossible for anybody else to do so. So he went on the attack.

He defended Paul's biblical arguments about Adam's sin and the resulting sinfulness of all people. No person could earn salvation on the basis of his own works. Augustine dismissed salvation by works as a possibility, and in the process worked toward a strong belief (again using Paul's words) in predestination.

While this belief influenced Catholic theology, Augustine's greatest legacy there was on the sacramental nature of salvation. For Augustine, sacraments are some of the ways God provides grace to believers. In fact, they're essential ways God provides grace, so in Catholic theology, you need to be connected to the church in order to have access to these key sources of grace. Baptism, in particular, is essential because it washes away the stain of original sin.

In Augustine's mind, baptism was part of a set of things—faith in Christ, repentance, baptism, the gift of the Holy Spirit—that all went together to remove the stain of original sin. But in succeeding generations, some Christians treated baptism as such an important source of grace that they lost sight of faith, repentance, and the Spirit as equally essential. Catholic Christians came to believe that grace also worked through penance, purgatory (an intermediate state of cleansing where a sinful Christian would go after he died until he was cleaned up enough for heaven), and other practices.

The church originally taught these practices as means by which a forgiven Christian pursues the process of becoming more Christlike. The idea was that salvation includes both freedom from the penalty of sin and (over time) increasing freedom from the habits of sin. But not everybody was interested in Christlikeness. Many just wanted to know the minimum requirements for getting into heaven. And in the generations after Augustine, lots of people came to think of the sacraments, penance, and other practices as means by which a person had to earn his way into heaven. For the average person, the idea of grace as a generous gift faded, and Christianity often seemed like a long to-do list. Some church leaders used this misunderstanding to acquire power over people's lives.

The Protestant Reformation (a thousand years later) eventually reemphasized Augustine's understanding that grace alone got a person into heaven and that grace was also essential to grow in Christlikeness. John Calvin in particular was drawn to his ideas about predestination. Augustine, then, provided the theological foundation not only for the Roman Catholic Church but for the churches of the Reformation as well.

AUGUSTINE'S DEATH AND HIS LEGACY

When a certain Count Boniface in North Africa rebelled against the Roman emperor, the emperor allied with the Vandals (who were at that time invading North Africa) to battle Count Boniface and subdue him. They succeeded, and Boniface surrendered to the imperial forces. Trouble was, the Vandals had no interest in making peace. They were there to conquer North Africa, and they proceeded to do so. Many refugees fled to the well-defended Hippo, and the Vandals laid siege to that city for eighteen months. During that siege Augustine—now seventy-six—contracted an illness. After three months he died, leaving behind a legacy of contributions to the Christian faith that put him among the most influential Christians in history.

He established the importance of grace over works as the

means for achieving salvation, which came at God's initiative to those he predestined to receive it. Augustine established the Catholic Church alone as the means for receiving this grace because the church controlled the sacraments. He laid out a philosophy of history that regarded all of history as a battle between the city of man and the city of God (we hear echoes of this view today in the "culture wars" played out in the Christian and secular media). He wrote the first autobiography and established the literary genre of confessional writing.

He also left a legacy that many modern evangelicals would balk at—would in fact repudiate. He was himself baptized when he became a believer as an adult, but he worked to regularize the practice of infant baptism. Why? Because he believed children were born in sin and would go to hell if they didn't receive the sacrament of baptism. This sacramental theology became one of the great dividing lines of the Reformation. Martin Luther taught believer's baptism theologically but didn't move his followers away from infant baptism. Calvin believed in the salvation of *elect* infants whether they were baptized or not. Much of the "Radical Reformation" (we'll get there eventually, don't worry) was born out of a repudiation of this practice and a return to what they called (and still call) "New Testament" baptism. Where you stand on this issue may have as much to do with your denominational background as anything, but this is the history of the beginning of infant baptism. You'll need to think for yourself what you believe about this issue.

But there is another legacy of Augustine that has cast a long shadow over the history of the church, one that has proved to be especially destructive. Remember the personal spiritual battle he waged with the sin of lust? After his conversion he never came to peace with human sexuality. The impact of this blind spot can be summed up in a phrase that continues to plague many churches today—that sex is dirty. It's not a biblical position to anyone who has read Song of Solomon. Yet the specter of sexuality has loomed over the church from that day to this, dividing people's spirits from their bodies and generating enormous guilt and shame among Christians everywhere.

Certainly the Bible forbids extramarital sex and exploiting other people for one's own gratification. But Augustine, like many Christian teachers after him, couldn't get his mind around the idea of sexuality as a gift from God to rejoice in. By treating all sexual desire as lust, he led even married people to feel guilty about enjoying sex (and led other people to ignore Christian teaching on sex entirely).

One purpose of this book is to answer the question, "How did the church get this way?" One response might be, "Go ask Augustine." He certainly had a lot to do with it. How did his contributions affect our themes?

People Like Us

Augustine was, by his own *Confessions*, a person like us. Hollywood screenwriters talk about a character's "story arc"—that means the events, responses, and solutions that every character of a drama moves through toward the resolution of the film. Augustine's life follows what might be called the conversion plot: He started one way, then absolutely transformed to go the other way, making his terrible early experiences into assets by recounting them honestly and repentantly. In that way, perhaps, his own story was much like Paul's.

But there may rest another aspect of his legacy that troubles the church and the world to this day. He never quite made it back from his "spirit = good, body = bad" dualism, and the impact of his struggle with lust upon millions who have sought to follow God in purity has not always been good. That "getting a good testimony" strategy? It isn't worth it. God used Augustine wonderfully, proving that he can make a mess into a marvel. But Augustine suffered terrible guilt for his early faults and failures, and to some extent he projected that guilt on all Christians who followed him.

The Body of Christ and the Human Institution

Augustine keenly felt the tension between the body of Christ and the human institution. He didn't want to become a bishop; he would have preferred the life of an Athens-style philosopher, spending his days in lively discussion with other educated minds. When he was pressed into service as the bishop of Hippo, he became more practical and more pessimistic. He could see the difference between the model of church in the New Testament and the reality of church in his era. To his credit, he remained faithful to the task of leadership that had been thrust upon him. At least he had the outlet of writing what he believed to be the ideal, though some would argue that it was not until much later that what Augustine wrote became widely believed and practiced.

Faith Versus Reason

Augustine believed that faith and reason are interactive: Reason precedes faith in that it takes a rational mind to recognize the truth, but faith precedes reason in that truth can only be understood through revelation. Augustine said, "Understanding is the reward of faith." But here's the key to what he meant: Neither faith nor reason, he believed, could be achieved by our *work*. Instead, he saw both faith *and* reason as being enabled by God's grace. Thus, logically, all of it comes as a result of God's grace.

Church + State = Very Bad Things

As a churchman of the Roman Empire in a time when the empire was crumbling and the church was becoming the only glue to hold it together, Augustine witnessed some terrible things and tried to accomplish some positive things. He recognized as well as anyone the difference between the body of Christ and the institution of the church controlled by (or at least much influenced by) the state. In *The City of God*, he stated his understanding of the difference and the need to keep that difference clearly in mind. It's a shame that many of those who read it in the Middle Ages misinterpreted what he was trying to say.

What About Missions?

Augustine became a missional pastor in the sense that he struggled regularly for the truth of the orthodox faith and refuted its enemies. The result was that many in North Africa came to the same faith he had by grace received. But while it might seem at times that he was a divider as he battled those he believed to be wrong, he was also a mender where it was possible. It was Augustine who helped pull the separated Tertullianist sect back into the larger church.

Ethics Optional?

Finally, were ethics optional? Not to Augustine. Ethical actions were the demonstration of the life of the believer. Surely you've heard it said that we are to "love the sinner and hate the sin." Augustine said that first. At least, he was the first to *write* it.

WANT TO KNOW MORE?

Why not go directly to the source? Don't ever be afraid to read the writings of great thinkers. They're considered great because they *communicate.* There are several good translations of Augustine's *Confessions*, and it reads as easily as most modern Christian autobiographies. Then you might want to go on to *The City of God*, but be forewarned that it demands a fair amount of historical background to really understand it. Other books that might be helpful are *Augustine: Wayward Genius* by David Bentley-Taylor (Grand Rapids, MI: Baker Book House, 1980), regarding his life, and *What Augustine Says*, edited by Norman Geisler (Grand Rapids, MI: Baker Book House, 1982), regarding his writings and positions on various issues. This second book is especially fascinating because you can see how—and often why—Augustine changed his mind.

5

Flames in the Darkness

PATRICK AND THE EARLY MIDDLE AGES

The Irish night was black — blacker than usual. It was Samhain (pronounced "sow'-en"), the druidic festival from which we've inherited Halloween. On this night, the dead were celebrated by utter darkness. All fires were to be extinguished as an act of religious devotion. Suddenly, on top of a high hill, a huge bonfire flamed into life, visible for miles around. Sacrilege! An invitation to doom! Who would have done such a shameful, catastrophic thing? Why, Patrick, of course, the one who would eventually be known as St. Patrick, patron saint of parades and green beer.

Did this actually happen? Who knows? It sounds a little too legendary for most scholars to even mention it. Most people don't even know the story, associating Patrick instead with leprechauns and driving all the snakes out of Ireland — which sounds a bit legendary too, doesn't it? But that there *was* a Patrick is clear, and we do know some things about him. Not the dates of his birth and death, although most fix these sometime in the late fourth to fifth centuries. Stripping away the legendary aspects of St. Paddy (do you imagine him wearing green the whole year round?) we still have the picture of a formidable man, one whose faith affected the whole of Ireland and from there the whole European continent.

PATRICK OF IRELAND
Born 383–415? Died 461–492?

Born not in Ireland but somewhere on the main British island, Patrick was kidnapped by Irish raiders and enslaved for six years as a herder. He escaped and returned home but felt called by God to return to Ireland as a missionary. Though opposed both by Druids and Arian priests, he planted orthodox churches and monasteries mostly on the northern and western sides of the island. So great was his impact that many legends grew up around him, but his true legacy was that, through his witness, Ireland relatively quickly became a land of Trinitarian Christian believers.

SAVED BY SLAVERY

Much of what we know of Patrick comes from his own *Declaration* (also called *The Confession of St. Patrick*). He was born into a ministerial family in Wales. His father was a deacon, his grandfather a presbyter. The date of his birth is hazy — some sources say as early as 383, some as late as 415. While he was raised a Christian, he apparently didn't give much attention to his faith as a child. The turning point of his life — early on, anyway — came when, at sixteen, he was kidnapped and enslaved by Irish raiders. He labored as a herder for six years. You might expect his attitude toward the Irish would be less than favorable. He wrote, however, that it was during this time that he began actually to depend on his faith and deepen his devotion to God. He wrote that he prayed every day.

At about the age of twenty-two, Patrick had a dream in which he was told to return to his people. He managed to escape, walking some two hundred miles before finding and boarding a ship. It took him to Europe, where he wandered for some time before he finally made it home. His family rejoiced, for they had thought him dead.

For most people, that might be the happy ending of the story. But Patrick had another dream: He saw an Irishman carrying a letter that read "The voice of Ireland." Then he heard the voices of many Irish pleading with him to return. Although not a trained minister, he returned to Ireland to carry the gospel to those who had enslaved him.

It would be an oversimplification to say that the island was completely without Christian witness. There were a number of Arian Christians mixed in with the Druids of the land, including many priests. Some of these opposed the Trinitarian gospel Patrick preached. He was attacked and persecuted, yet he persisted in establishing churches.

Some British Christians charged him with financial mismanagement, which is why he wrote *Declarations*—as a defense of his calling and his practice of ministry. In response to these charges, he refused to accept money or gifts, and returned those things that had been pressed upon him. He rededicated himself to establishing the faith, and he made a difference in people's lives through his consistent message and his persistence in preaching it. He wrote of baptizing thousands and of ordaining clergy. He evidently lived a very long life—March 17, 492 is given by some as the date of his death, although other sources hold he died as early as 461—and by the time of his passing, he was so revered that people began to celebrate the day as a holy day.

While he established many churches, most of these were staffed by a monastery of some sort nearby. The monastic church was the center of Irish Christianity, and when Irish missionaries influenced by Patrick began to travel to Britain and Europe, they followed this same monastic pattern. Columba, for example, took some monks with him and established a monastery on Iona, a small island off the coast of Scotland. From there they evangelized the ferocious Picts who dominated Scotland.

> Christ beside me, Christ before me, Christ behind me, Christ within me, Christ beneath me, Christ above me.
>
> FROM ST. PATRICK'S BREASTPLATE, TRADITIONALLY ATTRIBUTED TO ST. PATRICK

THE CHURCH AND THE WARRIOR CULT

The story of Patrick's bonfire may be legendary, but it's a metaphor for what the Holy Spirit accomplished in Ireland through him and others. There had been darkness, and from the flames of faith burning in a few committed individuals, light came to the island. Something similar happened to violent pagan tribes throughout Britain and Western Europe during the centuries after the Roman Empire collapsed and left those regions in a chaos of bloodshed. From the fourth to the tenth centuries AD, tribal groups (Irish, Picts, Scots, Saxons, Franks, and many more) that lived by subsistence farming, piracy, and war gradually encountered the gospel. When Roman order gave way in the fifth century, towns were pillaged and burned, and literacy became almost unknown in places like France. Then, ironically, it was the Irish and British monks—descendants of pirates and Druids—who kept copying old Roman books, including the Bible. Whether from the monasteries of the British Isles (the first real educational institutions in Europe) or from the Roman Catholic Church of southern Europe, there came to France and Germany a flood of missionaries that eventually Christianized Europe.

That's an interesting word: *Christianized*. It sounds like *pasteurized* or *vulcanized* or *simonized*—some kind of process to clean or patch or wax. It suggests a thin veneer of protective coating applied with a sprayer. And in many cases, the Christianization of Europe during the early Middle Ages (roughly AD 450–1050) didn't go very deep. It coated the warrior clans of Europe with a layer of surface religion but didn't always soak in deeply enough to change people's lives as fully as Jesus and the apostles called for.

Our culture today admires wealth, physical beauty, and fame. As Christians, many of us try to figure out how to be rich and Christian, and we love our Christian celebrities, especially if they're good looking. It's hard for us not to entangle the gospel with the surrounding culture's values. In a similar way, the tribes of early medieval Europe admired physical strength, courage, and success in battle. Just as we try to baptize our consumer culture, they baptized their warrior cult. (If you make a sword in the shape of a cross, it's a Christian symbol, isn't it?) Converting battle-hardened warlords at the heart level was no easier in fifth-century Germany than it had been for Constantine.

On the other hand, the Holy Spirit accomplished much in the six hundred years after Augustine and Patrick. With the collapse of the Roman Empire in the West, most people in western Europe lived at a bare subsistence level during this period. The monasteries filled the void in health care by inventing hospitals to provide basic care for the sick. They also developed the practice of adopting unwanted children. The pagan Romans had considered it appropriate to simply leave an unwanted baby outdoors until it died, but Christians decried this practice and eventually organized ways in which families or monasteries took in children with no questions asked.

It's hard for us to know how deep and accurate was the faith of the average Christian in medieval Europe. As literacy was rare in the early centuries and Bibles were extremely hard to come by because they had to be copied by hand, people had to depend on what their priests and their parents taught them. Priests in many places were poorly trained in the gospel. Also, pre-Christian customs and beliefs had deep roots. Just as we find it hard to disentangle the gospel from American consumerism and individualism, medieval Europeans grappled with a gospel mixed with warlord ethics and pagan practices.

Very likely there were many simple people with deep — if imperfectly informed — faith. There were some who went to monasteries for refuge from their violent world and for a real, intimate experience of Christ. Books like *The Imitation of Christ* (written later, in the fourteenth century, by Thomas à Kempis) bear witness to a genuine spiritual vitality in the monastic movement. The more powerful monasteries became infected with worldliness, but that was far from the whole story.

The church tried to moderate the violence of the pre-Christian warrior ethic by inventing the code of chivalry for knights. It also tried to address the extreme vulnerability of women. Neither of these efforts was anywhere near as successful as we would like, because church leaders were allured by power, wealth, and comfort, and because ordinary people were preoccupied with surviving poverty and danger. But faithful people were trying.

Some of the things the church tried in an effort to get people to take the faith seriously had consequences we can look back at with regret. For instance, how do you get a powerful, aggressive, barbaric warlord to give any thought to charitable works or fair treatment for his serfs? The church tried using the fear of hellfire and managed to make most medieval Christians profoundly afraid of hell. But fear, without the balancing awareness of love and grace, is of limited use in motivating people to follow Christ. We see that now, but it wasn't obvious to most well-meaning Christian leaders (as well as less well-meaning ones) in the Middle Ages.

There were also many brave missionaries. (Sometime you should Google Boniface of Germany and read about how he chopped down the tree of Thor.) Still, for all the heroic efforts of those who labored to Christianize Europe, Europe was no more thoroughly Christianized at the heart level than is modern America. The conflict between the cultural veneer of Christianity and the stubbornness of the human heart persisted.

This is a bridge chapter. In this book we're focusing on individuals who changed the church and caused it to become as it is. Patrick stands for the missionaries who evangelized Europe, most of whose names are lost. Equally lost are the names of admirable pastors, monks, and nuns in local areas, or the names of artists who invented the Gothic arch or the earliest forms of harmony. And for the most part, we know little of those who arose over and over in the church to reform abuses. (Francis of Assisi is one such who is worthy of your attention, and we'll get to him next.) Between the collapse of Rome and the invention of the printing press, legend and fact about individuals are hard to pull apart.

Still, we're going to look at several important shifts that occurred during the Middle Ages as the church grew from a radical movement into a vast institution. To understand the reform movements of the sixteenth century, we need to know about the schism between the eastern and western churches, the rise of the papacy, the development of the Holy Roman Empire, and the rise and expansion of Islam. They're all interrelated.

THE EAST-WEST SCHISM

The eastern church, which eventually came to be called the Orthodox Church, was centered in Constantinople (or Byzantium) from the time of Constantine until the fall of that city to the Muslims in 1453. Its fortunes rose and fell with those of the Byzantine Empire, which gives us a clue about the nature of the church. *Byzantine* is a word now used to describe a tangled web of confusing conspiracies, so complicated as to be nearly impossible to unravel. Since Constantine had made the church an integral part of his government and had controlled it, the church remained a captive of the succeeding emperors. Many of these were far from Christian in their behavior, but the church was in no real position to address these practical issues of morality. People who wanted deep devotion to Christ turned increasingly to monasteries, which were supposed to be above the obsession with power and money (although they failed at this as often as they succeeded), and to mystical forms of prayer. They sought freedom from worldliness in prayer, fasting, solitude, and silence.

After the empire divided and the western half collapsed under the onslaught of warrior tribes, the relationships between the eastern and the western churches grew progressively worse. The official divorce came slowly, and seemed (like most divorces) to be the result of petty bickering over small issues, based upon a long history of poor communication. We've already seen the reasons for this—the churches of the East and West *thought* differently. They spoke different languages (Latin versus Greek). They viewed themselves differently.

One of the big problems was the question of authority. The western church claimed primacy of position for the bishop of the Church of Rome, the pope. The eastern churches regarded Rome as only one of five leading churches, the so-called Patriarchates, the others being in Jerusalem, Antioch, Alexandria, and Constantinople. The idea of bending the knee to a single ruler of the church didn't sit well with these other leaders at all. The whole idea of "whoever desires to become great among you, let him be your servant" (Matthew 20:26) didn't make much of an impression on church leaders of the time.

So the West and East split apart. One factor was the increasing power of the papacy and its insistence upon the existence of a "Holy Roman Empire." When, during the Crusades, knights of the western church sacked Constantinople as if it were a Muslim city, well, it wasn't a high point in East-West relations.

It's hard to date when the split occurred. The crowning of Charlemagne as the Holy Roman Emperor in AD 800 was one nail in the coffin of their dead relationship. Another crisis came when the pope added "and the Son" to the Nicene Creed, and the East objected to the pope's changing the doctrine of the Holy Spirit. Really, a kind of cold war continued between the two churches from 800 until 1054, when the pope and the patriarchs excommunicated each other.

THE HOLY ROMAN EMPIRE

Charlemagne—Charles the Great—was the first person in hundreds of years to reunite under one rule much of the old Western Roman Empire. He received the kingdom of the Franks from his father and expanded it mightily. He defeated (and converted) the Saxons in the far north of Europe. He drove down halfway into Spain (against the Muslim rulers there), as well as defeated the Lombards of Italy, who surrounded and threatened the pope in Rome. He lived a long time, and rarely during that time was there peace everywhere in his empire. But Charlemagne was a big man (about six feet four) among much smaller people, and he apparently enjoyed a good fight.

Because he took the pressure off the pope of the time by subduing the Lombards (and because that pope, Leo III, wanted to clearly announce the freedom of the Western Empire from the East), Charlemagne was crowned the Holy Roman Emperor. He apparently didn't know he was being so honored while it was happening, nor did he want the title. But it served the pope's purposes. It also set in motion a confusing institution and title that plagued Europe for almost a thousand years. What did "the Holy Roman Empire" *mean*? Whatever the current emperor and pope wanted it to, apparently. This so-called union of Christendom under a single earthly ruler became a constant cause of spite, jealousy, and war in the years to come. It's a maze to follow the title through history as it was passed around from one great family to another. In that way, it was much like its ecclesiological parallel — the papacy itself.

THE RISE (AND FALL?) OF THE PAPACY

We've seen that the Western Empire crumbled under the attacks of "barbarians" such as the Goths and the Vandals (interesting, isn't it, how those names persist into the present with different meanings?). While the empire's government dissolved, the church remained. The tribes gradually became Christian, and the Latin church became the link that bound them together. Rome no longer controlled the landscape militarily, but the Roman bishop maintained great influence, functioning more and more as a political leader, not just a spiritual guide. The role grew until the Latin church regarded this leader as more than the first among bishops. Rather, he became the father — the "Papa" — of all. For a while his influence extended north to the edge of the conquests of Christian kings (that's why Charlemagne's later conquests were so helpful), west through Spain and up to England, and south through North Africa to the desert. But half of that territory was to be wiped away by the explosion of Islam.

We'll see below how that happened. There was a point when it appeared that Islam would sweep across Europe, erasing the church entirely. The Battle of Tours, however, in the 700s, stopped Islam's progress and pushed it back into Spain. The very existence of Islam, however, called into question the central tenet of Christendom — that Christ was the head of the *world's* governments, as well as of the kingdom of heaven.

Ultimately, the pressure grew until Pope Urban II called for the First Crusade against the Muslims in 1096. It's an understatement to say the legacy of these wars with the Muslims continues with us today.

The papacy was, in effect, a government without an army. That's why the popes (the smart ones, anyway) made alliances with the powerful earthly kings that surrounded them. Often these alliances proved helpful. Sometimes they proved cumbersome. And sometimes the political rivalries of the earthly kings had terribly negative effects on the papacy. Sometimes the popes themselves were not people of high moral character — or even, in the view of some, really Christians at all. It's easy to see, then, why many in the church regarded the papacy with resentment and suspicion. Some groups of Christians even rebelled. You might call these minireformations or simply attempts at decentralization. The Irish and British churches, for example, held out against papal oversight until the mid-600s, and even after that they were known to appeal to Constantinople when they didn't like a ruling from Rome.

Some popes responded violently to challenges to their authority. Some groups of dissenters were officially suppressed, with thousands killed. The Albigenses, or Cathari, were a heretical group that held views similar to the Manichaeans (see chapter 4). Having determined that crusades could be effective, Innocent III directed a crusade against the Albigenses, during which thousands of men, women, and children were mutilated and murdered. While it wasn't the first time that charges of heresy resulted in deaths, it may be that this one set the pattern for later responses to the Protestant Reformation. It was a terrible precedent. By the way — remember Innocent III's name. He features prominently in our next chapter.

It could be argued, of course, that in this warlike stance the medieval church only mirrored its Islamic competition across the Mediterranean Sea. Certainly the Muslims did violence in the name of Allah. Should we have expected a more Christlike response from popes and kings who felt physically threatened? Even if we did, it wouldn't change history.

THE RISE AND EXPANSION OF ISLAM

A forty-year-old camel trader who had been exposed to both Judaism and a form of Christianity felt the call to "recite." Over a period of about twenty years, Muhammad dictated the suras, or chapters, of the Koran. While the people of his native Mecca didn't believe him and persecuted him, he continued to obey the heavenly voice until at last he was forced to run for his life to Medina. There he found believers, became a political ruler, organized an army, and returned to conquer Mecca. Muhammad did not believe in any separation between heavenly rule and earthly control. There was one God, Allah, and he, Muhammad, was his prophet.

Muhammad died in 632. Within one hundred years of his death, Muhammad's armies had conquered all of the Middle East as well as Christian Egypt, Christian North Africa, and Christian Spain. In 732, that important Battle of Tours took place. The battle was won by Frankish Christians, blocking Islam's further advance into western Europe. If it had turned out differently, we might all be speaking Arabic.

That defeat didn't stop the Muslims in the East, however. Muslim armies rolled across present-day Pakistan and on through what we know as Bangladesh. Muslims carried their faith by boat to the vast archipelago we know as Indonesia. All the while, Islamic armies in the Middle East kept hammering northward against the Byzantine Empire. This they continued to do until at last Constantinople itself fell, was renamed Istanbul, and became the center of the Turkish Empire. (Technically, the Crusades belong to chapter 6 on the High Middle Ages, AD 1000–1400, but because the Christian-Muslim wars began in the early Middle Ages, we're treating the whole conflict here.)

During this period, when civilized life (economic standard of living, literacy rates, and so forth) in the Christian West was at low ebb, Muslims experienced their golden age. The caliphs of Baghdad ruled empires as vast as those of the Babylonian and Persian kings of the past. Muslim scholars kept alive the thoughts of Plato and Aristotle, and pushed the development of mathematics. Muslims pioneered military strategies and technologies, which they employed against the cumbersome European knights sent down to attack them by crusading popes. While Islam, like the Christian church, divided in a great split and then subdivided into multiple denominations and varieties, the Muslim presence had come to stay.

The impact of Islam on Christianity went beyond military rivalry and a kind of religious mirror image. The Christian crusaders learned much from Muslims—some good, some bad. They carried back with them to Europe a taste for certain Eastern luxuries: edibles and scents and textiles that furthered trade. They formed military/religious brotherhoods like the Knights Templar, who became financiers once their swords were no longer much needed. The crusaders returned with ideas that prompted thoughts among Christian scholars that harkened back to the theological debates of the fifth and sixth centuries. Controversies among Christian thinkers flared anew. Did Islam and the Crusades stimulate the rebirth of thought in the West we call the Renaissance? It sure helped.

This is a lot of history to cover at a single bound. With all these epic movements, battles, empires, and political scheming, why begin this bridge chapter with Patrick? Perhaps because he is truly representative of the *most* important movement in Christianity—its continued spread from one heart to another throughout the entire period. Yes, in many cases, the Christianity spread by political declaration and military conquest was less than genuine. But in many places—in Ireland, Scotland, Germany, Scandinavia, as well as up into present-day Russia—there were genuine conversions to the way of Christ Jesus. While there was much failure in both eastern and western churches during this period, there was also much good—flames in the darkness. The simple faith of the apostles was spread in the same way they themselves had spread it in the first century.

When I was a boy, the number one television show was *Bonanza*. It aired on Sunday night, and I wondered if my dad didn't orchestrate moving the evening worship service up an hour just so he could get home in time to watch it. It began with a map of Nevada that caught fire in the center and burned to the outward edges of the screen. I've often thought that was a good model for what happened with the spread of Christianity. It began with a flame that burned outward. While in the center, the embers of the faith may have dwindled, at the edge of the old Roman Empire the flame burned brightly, changing people's lives. Yes, there was a lot of "show" Christianity practiced by those who saw the declaration of Christian faith as a social and political necessity. That still happens, doesn't it? But it doesn't change this essential fact: The Christian faith spread from true believers to new believers—and they carried it still farther. Who were these faithful missionaries? People like Patrick. People like us.

People Like Us

Patrick was certainly human. While he did his best to refute the charge of mishandling money, it stung him enough to cause him to write his *Declaration* and to change the way he dealt with money from that time forward. He was persecuted for his faith and responded to that persecution as most of us would, with anger and defensiveness. But his spirit must have been such that people were attracted to him, for he left behind many who loved him and, more importantly, many who loved Christ. Perhaps we would do well to focus upon the simple testimony of his life choice—to respond to God's call to return to the very people who had enslaved him as a boy and to give them the good news that had sustained him during his captivity.

The Body of Christ and the Human Institution

The early medieval church had become a very human institution that provided political unity in a fractured continent. Feudal lords used it to bind vassals to them and to enforce their "divine right" to rule. Like the lords they worked with, the popes developed a pragmatic political sense. The goal of Christendom—a continent united under the single banner of Christ—was more or less accomplished. But where in all this was the church still the body of Christ?

A quick answer might be "everywhere." While there was much misunderstanding of Christ's kingdom and many who used its organization only for their own selfish purposes, everywhere the church went there were some—like Patrick—who became totally committed to the faith. Whether few or many, these were like that legendary fire in the black night, bringing light wherever they went.

Faith Versus Reason

Reason was very much a part of early medieval Christianity, but the *style* of reason reflected the context of the times. One example is the thinking of Anselm of Canterbury, a French priest who traveled to England when the Normans invaded in 1066 and who became archbishop of Canterbury. In his *Cur Deus Homo?* (*Why the God-Man?*) Anselm explained Christ's atonement for our sin in a uniquely medieval way. While many evangelicals today know only the *substitutionary* theory (Christ became the substitute for our sin) Anselm voiced the *satisfaction* theory: God the Father was like a feudal lord whose honor had been besmirched by our sin. Christ's atonement was needed to provide satisfaction for this slight. Does that seem a small difference? There are actually two other major theories of the Atonement, and reams of paper have been eaten up in debate over the differences.

My point here is that reason was not dead during this period. It's just that most people didn't have the luxury of getting educated and exploring ideas. In its best moments, the church was focused on helping people in practical ways, providing health care and bringing simple and barely surviving peasants out of paganism and into heaven. And when the Renaissance came, the "new reason" was just as specific to its time as Anselm's writings had been to *his* time.

Church + State = Very Bad Things

We could spend many pages talking about the negative effects of the relationship between church and state during this period. The popes ran the church and played politics, and the church traded treasure in heaven for the wealth and power of this world. In fact, control of heaven became a potent political tool for the popes during this time—the most potent. If a king got too out of line, the pope could threaten to excommunicate him, to put him outside the communion of God and thus damn him to hell. Whether the king believed this himself or not, his people often did, and an excommunicated king or duke or whatever could find his armies melting away for fear that they, too, would be excommunicated. The popes played this trump card often—for earthly political gain. There were, of course, good popes. They just weren't perfect. And the institutions of the time made it less likely for humble, wise men to rise to the papacy.

The church's flaws were so apparent that many of the faithful saw clearly the need for reform. That was coming first from those who remained firmly within the Catholic Church, then from those who were either put out of it or walked away.

What About Missions?

We began this chapter with a missionary, but during this period missions were largely misplaced. How can we say that? Certainly the conversion of all those pagan tribes was a major accomplishment, even though the gospel got muddled with pre-Christian ideas and practices. But the more people thought in terms of Christendom, Christ's kingdom on earth as a political reality, the more missions were treated as a political rather than personal enterprise. The wars with Islam, for instance, were aimed first at protecting Europe from conquest and forced conversion and then at liberating formerly Christian (or partly Christian) territories from Muslim rule, thus the effort to retake Jerusalem and the Holy Land. The Crusades had a missionary intent, but they were hardly the proudest moment of Christian missions.

Ethics Optional?

We could spend another hundred pages listing the failures of Christian leaders during this period. Charlemagne, the model Christian king of the Middle Ages, did as much as anyone, perhaps, to Christianize Europe. After all, he conquered the Saxons and forced them to surrender and be baptized (note that military surrender and religious conversion were treated as one and the same). Despite being the pope's protector and eventually the Holy Roman Emperor, despite being big and handsome and victorious and all the other things that would have made him a great leading man today, Charlemagne had ethical problems related to marriages, children, and such. His daughters ran wild, yet he never seemed to notice. He was more humane to those he defeated than Constantine had been, usually putting them in monasteries rather than killing them, but this paragon of Christian virtue (in image, at least) was no paragon of Christian virtue. And this was the *model* king. Let's just say that there were terrible ethical failures within the early medieval church, and the people noticed.

For the vast majority of Christians, ethics weren't optional. The monastic rules emphasized ethics, and before they became too wealthy and powerful, the monasteries were a positive force. As they do today, preachers hammered on the people about doing good, sometimes too much. The church instituted the rule of celibacy for priests in response to problems of priestly sexual immorality and financial misconduct, such as trying to leave the wealth of one's church to one's children. Clearly there were people at the top trying to enforce Christian morality. There were many more who were doing the best they could in monasteries and parishes. The first effective reformers sought to reform the church from the inside. One of the greatest—and most humble—was Francis of Assisi, who we will discuss in the next chapter.

WANT TO KNOW MORE?

We've covered a lot of time in these brief pages, and a lot of people. My students sometimes grumble about having to learn names and dates from Christian history, but I always remind them that each of these names belongs to an actual *person*—even if, like Patrick, there are obviously legends attached to them. Believe me, there are many, many other names I would have liked to mention. I suggest a good history of Christianity as a place to begin to learn more. Kenneth Scott Latourette's *A History of Christianity: Beginnings to 1500* (San Francisco: HarperSanFrancisco, 1975) is deep and detailed. Bruce L. Shelley's *Church History in Plain Language* (Nashville: Thomas Nelson, 1996) is shorter and less detailed, but is extremely readable, as its title indicates.

Is There a Right Way to Know God?

FRANCIS AND AQUINAS

Francis of Assisi wanted to be like Jesus—and he was. It is impossible to read about him without loving him—or, at the very least, loving the Christlike life he struggled daily to lead. In the movie *Brother Sun, Sister Moon* (1972), Italian director Franco Zeffirelli turned Francis into something like a 1960s flower child, a spiritual hippie who stripped away dead traditions along with his clothes and rebelled against the system through peace and love. Zeffirelli did Francis an injustice, for the flower children of the sixties became the "me" generation of the seventies and eighties and traded their idealism for material wealth. Francis was, indeed, a slacker rich kid who became high on the Spirit of God, but he lived out his commitment throughout his short life and thereby changed the church and the world. All Francis wanted was to be like Jesus. His life certainly reminds me of the way Jesus lived and loved.

Thomas Aquinas was another rich kid who became a man of God against his parents' wishes. His approach to God, however, was not through public love but through private thought. His masterwork, the *Summa Theologiae*, has set the standard for every systematic theology written since, and he changed the church through the glittering brilliance of his mind. It is interesting to note, however, that toward the end of his life he had a worship experience that caused him to end his scholarly career and to count everything he had written as nothing against the glories God had permitted him to see.

THE HIGH MIDDLE AGES (AD 1000–1400)

The blossoming of art and learning that was the Renaissance didn't just start up one day out of the blue. It was a couple of centuries in coming. While the Renaissance is typically dated from the fifteenth century, the seeds of the new learning began germinating as far back as the thirteenth. Universities (assemblies of scholars in various large cities) began forming in the thirteenth century and began to resurrect the works of Aristotle and other long-lost classics, thereby laying the foundation for the new ideas the Renaissance spread around. The big shifts in theology came with things like the distribution of the Greek New Testament (which waited upon the printing press in the fifteenth century), but these changes in perspective built upon the work of the medieval scholastics.

In fact, it has been argued persuasively that the Renaissance was partly a response to the Black Death that wiped out a third of Europe's population in the fourteenth century. The Black Death had a huge effect on church history because many people became disillusioned with faith in God, and that fueled the secularization of the fifteenth century. "Man is the measure of all things" is what many people concluded after they rebuilt their society from a plague that made AIDS look like the common cold.

The High Middle Ages was a glorious time to be a Christian artist. The Greek and Roman technical expertise in the arts had been largely lost when the Roman Empire fell, and early medieval painters of icons and illuminated manuscripts had to do their best to copy the works of older masters without the masters' training. But once the European economy picked up after AD 1000, people invested money and time in Christian art. They built cathedrals, wrote poetry, and invented new techniques in painting. They used an array of visual arts — from stone masonry to tapestries to theater — to convey Bible stories to people who couldn't read. Church musicians invented harmony to express the Trinitarian idea of different voices singing one unified song. Dante's *The Divine Comedy*, an epic poem written in the fourteenth century, contains an immense amount of reasoning about the nature of spiritual growth, the relationship of church and state, sin understood as disordered love, and on and on.

Before we can understand the Renaissance, then, we need to understand the High Middle Ages. Francis and Aquinas were far from the only heroes of this period, but they placed the stamp of their very different personalities on this time to the glory of God. Through their lives and writings, they set different but highly relevant examples of how to seek God. While they were born out of the same confusion of a politically corrupt and secularized Roman Catholic Church, their responses to the same set of problems were different. Does the God who made the vast diversity of our world take pleasure in our differences? Or is there a one-size-fits-all prescription for knowing him that has applied, does apply, and will apply to each person in every generation?

FRANCIS THE LOVER

When you think of a Catholic saint, you may think immediately of Francis without even knowing that you are. He's that modest figure with a funny haircut who, in his statues, bends slightly to one side while he talks to the birds perched on his shoulder. Francis is the epitome of sainthood — he was acknowledged as a saint even during his lifetime. (But he managed to duck the conceit that praise must have prompted within him. Of course, what would you expect from a *true* saint?)

He certainly didn't begin his life in a saintly manner. He was a normal boy with normal interests and passions, born to privilege in a wealthy Italian family. He was a younger child in a large family, meaning that he would always be well cared for but would not be among the family decision makers. His father was away on business when he was born, and his mother named him John, evidently in hopes that he would one day become a great leader of the church. That was prophetic but certainly not a part of his father's plans. When Francis's father returned from France, he angrily renamed his son after the land he'd been visiting when the child was born.

FRANCIS OF ASSISI (FRANCESCO GIOVANNI DI BERNARDONE)
1182–1226

Francis was born to a prominent (and tight-fisted) textile merchant of the proud Italian city of Assisi. A playful, irresponsible youth who had little interest in school, he became one of the greatest of the saints of the Roman Catholic Church through his absolute devotion to poverty, chastity, and obedience to Christ. More, perhaps, than any other saint, he took up the cause of the downtrodden and sick, identifying with them and working beside them. He did all this with great joy that lifted the spirits of those around him and summoned their best. The Order of the Friars Minor (Franciscans) grew up around him, made him their model, and, through imitation of his imitation of Christ, changed the world.

Francis was a leader, but not necessarily because he tried to be. He led by doing. He was good at athletics, popular with girls, fun to be around—and generally worthless. His father gave him money, but he had the bad habit (to his father, anyway) of spending it lavishly on his friends or giving it away to the poor. Consider this: A good-looking, good-loving, goof-off kid; a God-fearing but more husband-fearing mother; a miserly, explosive-tempered father—you can almost see a TV drama plot developing, can't you? The story became very dramatic indeed, but bad relations between the father and son were interrupted for a year by war.

It wasn't a big war or a long one. Assisi's rival city was Perugia. The two towns hated one another and fought frequent skirmishes. These battles held about the emotional importance of a rivalry football game—the young men fought, there was much emphasis on pomp and color, and the spoils of victory were mostly bragging rights. Still, people got killed and prisoners were taken. Francis was captured and spent about a year in a Perugian jail. When he finally returned to his hometown, he was a changed young man—more reflective and confused about his future. His friends tried to pull him back into their round of parties, but his heart wasn't in it.

VISIONS

A knight invited Francis to travel to battle in another area, and he prepared to go. He dreamed of a hall full of shields, each with a cross on it, and a voice told him, "These shall be for your soldiers." He woke up believing he was to be a great prince, and he set out in high spirits with the knight. Then he had another dream, in which the voice told him to turn back to Assisi. He was obviously a great believer in dreams, for he obeyed.

On one occasion, he was traveling across a field when he saw a leper begging. He recoiled in horror and rode away, but then he turned back, dismounted, and embraced the leper. He gave the man all the money he had with him. He later called this chance meeting a turning point. He was putting actions to the stirrings in his heart. He made a pilgrimage to Rome and, while waiting to see the pope, noticed all around him beggars of every kind. He traded his rich robes for those of a beggar and gave *this* man all of his money. He then stood with the others and begged all day, experiencing poverty for the first time. When he returned to Assisi, it was with a new understanding of the effect of money on the people around him — and of Jesus' words about the poor.

He took to praying frequently in some of the broken-down chapels in the countryside around Assisi. As he knelt one February day before a statue of Jesus, the statue came alive and said, "Rebuild my church, for you can see that it's fallen into ruin." With our wide-angle view of the church's problems, we might easily jump to an abstract, worldwide view of Francis's calling. The church as a whole *did* need rebuilding. Francis, however, took the words literally, for he could see how the chapel around him was broken down. He set out to rebuild it but made a mistake. He went home to his father's house, collected up many yards of his father's expensive cloth, put it on a horse, and took it to another town to sell it, horse included. He took the gold he received back to the priest in charge of the tumbledown chapel and tried to give it to the man. The priest refused. Frustrated, Francis threw the gold to the ground. Then he went off to hide in a cave for a month because he knew his father would explode.

He was right. When at last he returned to Assisi, he was in terrible shape, ragged and skinny from lack of food. His father grabbed him, tied him up, and took him home. There he first beat him, then locked him in a closet. Francis's mother let him out the next time his father was gone, and he left home, never to return. His father had gone to the chapel to pick up the gold, but he also charged his son with theft and wanted to legally disown him. Francis accepted this, taking off all his clothes and handing them to his father. "From this point," he said, "I will only call my father in heaven 'Father.'"

COLLECTING BROTHERS

Francis began to travel, preaching and singing of Jesus. Robbers beat him up, stripped him, and threw him into the snow, but he survived and managed to find some rags to wear. Then he went about what he believed to be his task, begging in the streets of Assisi for stones he could use to rebuild the chapels. He made a powerful impression on the townspeople. Several of the wealthy, educated men of Assisi gave what they had to the poor and followed him. When the Benedictine monks gave him one of the chapels he had rebuilt, he and his followers built huts around it and made it their home.

When eleven men had joined him, Francis realized he needed to provide some organization, so he wrote down a rule for them to follow, as other monastic orders had. His was very simple, however: a vow of chastity, poverty, and service to others. Francis got this straight from the teachings of Jesus without any teachings of the church fathers in between. It obviously wasn't his managerial skills that attracted others to follow his path. He just set out to live as much as he could like Jesus, and others recognized that and responded.

Eventually he felt the need to get official approval for his group, so he led them to Rome and appealed to the pope for permission to form an order. This was Pope Innocent III, who had sent a crusade against the heretics in France (see chapter 5). Innocent wasn't sure Francis's order was a good idea. The vow of poverty bothered members of his Curia (heads of departments that ran the Catholic Church), who thought it was irresponsible. Innocent III approved Francis's order, however, as he did another saint's appeal to begin a new order. He is credited, then, for establishing both the Franciscans and the Dominicans, two of the most important orders in Catholic history. He is also accounted one of the most powerful and influential popes in medieval history—so we might want to take a moment to get to know him better.

INNOCENT III

Innocent became pope at thirty-seven—a mighty young age for such a powerful office—and immediately took action to enforce his views of the role of the pope among the world's rulers. He intervened in the politics of just about every country in Europe and eventually Asia, too. He took control of the election of the Holy Roman Emperor when two emperors were elected at the same time and went to war with one another. In the process, he pulled the kings of Europe under his control.

He forced the rulers of the small states around Rome to yield to him as political leader. He put King John of England (and the whole English nation) under interdict when John fought his choice for archbishop of Canterbury. John gave in, and Innocent III was ceded ultimate authority over the English crown, with John as his vassal. When John's barons later forced him to sign the Magna Carta, Innocent III overturned it, saying that it had been forced upon John and was not of his will. (Well, duh!)

Probably Innocent's most notable failures were his crusades. The crusade against the Albigensian Christians turned into a bloodbath; the barons of southern France used it as an excuse to conquer territory. It's impossible to know, but some suggest as many as fifty thousand lives were lost in this internal crusade. Even worse, it legitimized the use of death as means of "saving" the souls of heretical sinners, giving rise to the Inquisition that followed soon thereafter.

It's the other crusade Innocent launched, however, that gets the most press. After the failure of the Third Crusade (the one Richard the Lion-Hearted fought in), Innocent launched the ill-fated Fourth Crusade. The crusaders didn't have enough money to pay the leaders of Verona to sail them to the Holy Land, so the Veronese offered them a deal: Conquer for Verona a nearby city and they would win free passage. The crusaders did so, then got offered another deal: Conquer *Constantinople* and get another ten thousand crusaders added to their number. So they conquered Constantinople. Pillaged and raped for four days. Never did make it to the Holy Land.

Innocent III was appalled. He excommunicated the crusaders who participated and said some really terrible things about them. However, since the damage was already done, he thought he'd use this opportunity to reunify the eastern church with the western. Under his control, of course. He appointed Latin bishops to go take over the eastern churches. It didn't work. In fact, it just put more distance between the Latin and Greek churches. I'll bet you're surprised by that, aren't you?

FRIARS MINOR

To his credit, however, Innocent III gave Francis permission to start his new order. Francis called it the Friars Minor — perhaps just to keep the group humble. Eventually he divided up Europe and sent his friars out two-by-two. Wherever they traveled, more people joined the order. In addition, a wealthy young woman from Assisi named Clare decided she, too, wanted to join. Francis accepted her as the first of the Poor Ladies — an order that eventually became known as the Poor Clares.

The order continued to grow. Francis continued to resist organization. Then, when he finally managed to make a trip to the Holy Land to convert the Muslims, he left his order in the care of several followers. His Holy Land trip was thrilling — he marched straight into the camp of the sultan and was captured, then won the man's confidence and friendship. Those traveling with him explained that he was finally kicked out of the camp when the sultan began to fear he would, indeed, convert the Muslim soldiers. Perhaps Francis could have had a genuinely powerful impact upon Islam, but he was called home by terrible news: His simple order was being changed.

There was now a huge new house for the friars to live in. Francis wouldn't enter it. There was a school under Franciscan guidance. Francis didn't believe in book learning when a friar could learn all he needed to know in prayer and in the streets. Some who were joining the order wanted to forgo the vow of poverty, and others could see that absolute poverty would be detrimental to the order's growth and initiatives. That, to Francis, had been the whole point. But it seemed clear to his early associates that the order had grown too big for informal governance, and they had only attempted to supply what Francis would not. It was a bitter pill to swallow, but Francis resigned as the head of the order he had founded and that bore his name. He had realized the truth—that the order had outgrown him—and he wanted it to be the order God intended. There was still much to reform within the church. He didn't want to get in the way.

FREE AGAIN

It was a good choice for Francis. Freed of the administrative responsibility, he was able to return to doing the simple ministry he loved. He thought of a new way to celebrate Christmas: What if they were to set up a manger scene, using real animals like sheep, goats, and cows? That manger scene in your local church last Christmas was one of Francis's innovations.

Another innovation that pained him much, and that his brothers didn't reveal until after his death, was that Francis received the *stigmata*—the five wounds of Christ in the hands, feet, and side—some years before he died. Stigmata are a very controversial subject that has been overworked by modern horror movies. It is interesting to note that Francis was apparently the first person on record to receive these wounds.

Eventually he became sick, and he was carried hurriedly and under guard past that pesky city of Perugia. Had he died there, the Perugians would have had the right to claim his bones as relics, something they apparently had already done with the body of Innocent III, who had died there ten years before and whose body had *not* been returned to Rome. Francis was already being venerated as a saint before he died. He was elevated to sainthood almost immediately. It's easy to understand why.

DOMINIC

Francis was a lover. He wasn't Jesus; he just wanted to be as much *like* Jesus as he could be. In pursuit of that goal, he emphasized the scriptural attributes of Jesus that he found most appealing. Another man of the same time wanted just as much to be like Jesus, but he saw the Lord in a different way. Dominic de Guzmán became very concerned for the Albigenses when he passed through southern France. He saw the need for committed preachers who would engage the heretics' minds in a common, understandable way and then persuade them to return to the true faith. To do this effectively, he felt education was critical, so, unlike Francis, he saw a place for scholarship. Five years after approving the Franciscan order, Innocent III approved the Order of Preachers, who were eventually known as Dominicans. While Dominic was an interesting man himself, his order trained a leader who was to have far more direct influence upon the future of the church than he. One of these is our next study: the father of systematic theology, Thomas Aquinas.

THOMAS THE THINKER

Thomas was born to a noble family in about 1225, just a little before the death of Francis. He was directly related to the Holy Roman Emperor (who had been put in place by Innocent III). His father was a count and his mother an even higher status countess. His uncle was the abbot of Monte Cassino, a great monastery south of Rome (which you may have heard of because it was the site of a lengthy and bloody battle during World War II). The family plan was for Thomas to eventually succeed his uncle in this role, so he was sent to school there when he was very young.

Monte Cassino belonged to the "old" church — it was very much a part of the status quo. Thomas's uncle saw that the boy was brilliant and suggested to his family that he deserved a much better education. (That's what happens when you quickly demonstrate you know more than your teachers.) He was sent first to Cologne and then to Paris for further schooling and became acquainted with the activities of these new, revolutionary Catholics, the Dominicans and Franciscans. When he suddenly took the black habit of the Dominican order, his parents took action. They had his brother lock him up. For a year or two.

THOMAS AQUINAS (THOMAS OF AQUIN)
ca. 1225–1274

The greatest of the philosopher theologians known as the Scholastics, Aquinas wrote the ultimate rational systematic theology for the Roman Catholic Church — the *Summa Theologiae*. Born to a highly placed family and favored with every early advantage, he chose to join the poor Dominican order and to give his life to scholarship. Although offered high office, he refused it, preferring instead to stick with his books. He made a consistent harmonization of Aristotle's thought with that of the church, which earned for him the title "Doctor Angelicus" and "Doctor Universalis." Of the thirty-three recognized Doctors of the Church, he is held in the highest esteem.

The story is that his brothers even tried to tempt him with a prostitute, but he sent her away. The family then offered to buy him the cushy post of archbishop of Naples. If you see the Roman Catholic Church as monolithic, the family response may seem to be an overreaction. But the Franciscans and Dominicans were still very new, and to his parents it might have seemed that Thomas was trying to join some crazy cult. After all, in 1232 (when Thomas was just seven) the pope had put the Dominicans in charge of the Inquisition. Perhaps his family was genuinely worried about what their brilliant son and brother was getting himself into.

THE INQUISITION

The Inquisition is the ultimate dark blot on the church's record that some non-Christians will point to as a primary indicator of the deadly hypocrisy of Christians. How could the sacrificial love of the carpenter of Galilee lead to tortures and executions? It's a fair question.

First, there wasn't just one Inquisition; there were a series of them that began with the crusade against the Albigenses. Innocent III's original intent appears to have been to regularize actions against supposed heretics. For centuries there had been opposition to the Roman Catholic Church by one group or another, and individual rulers of the various states had taken their own action against those they termed heretical—whether they really were or not. Innocent wanted these accusations and actions brought firmly under the control of the church.

Besides, there were sections of southern France where the Albigensian heresy was openly celebrated, and the so-called Christian rulers over these towns and villages refused to take action against their people. It was a trip through this area that had stirred in Dominic the need to rescue these people back to the faith by earnest, educated preaching. He tried his plan, but the people wouldn't convert. Innocent III grew impatient and offered the lands to whatever "Christian" nobles would conquer them. It's cynical to say this, but a number of rulers suddenly got religion. The race was on. The crusade lasted twenty years — and it didn't focus upon the Albigenses alone. The followers of Peter Waldo also came under the sword. (I know you're thinking, "Where's Waldo?" Just get it out of your system, and we'll go on.)

The Waldensians, followers of Peter Waldo, were an early Protestant group. Waldo's conversion experience took place in 1174 — three centuries before the Reformation — but the views of Waldo and his followers appear very similar to the doctrinal statements of many evangelical groups today. One inquisitor contemptuously enumerated these beliefs: The Waldensians rejected ecclesiastical authority, believing it was not based upon the New Testament; they rejected or reinterpreted the sacraments; they rejected feast days as human creations; they set themselves up as an alternative church without a priest; they denied purgatory; their leaders were expected to travel and evangelize; and they performed missionary preaching in the local language with a strong emphasis on the New Testament. This last was most bothersome to the inquisitors and led the church to forbid translations of the Latin Scriptures into local languages for fear that those reading the New Testament would reject established church beliefs.

As the Albigensian Crusade continued, Innocent III and the popes after him grew steadily more troubled by the disorganized state of local inquisitions and determined to unify them under a single papal authority. The Dominicans, primarily, were commissioned with responsibility for determining and punishing heresy. The original sentence for heretics was not death but "death"—the church accounted them dead and confiscated their lands, and this only after a lengthy process.

But once someone was charged with heresy, they had a hard time disproving the accusation. Their trial could—and often did—involve torture. Church law determined that those accused of heresy could only be tortured *once*; however, such torture could be continued until a confession was obtained. You can readily see how this clause could be abused. The torturers would just continue the torment, rather than stop it and be unable to begin again later.

It wasn't long before the sentence of a heretic was literal death, usually by burning. When the Inquisition condemned a heretic as beyond help, it turned him or her over to the secular authorities to be put to death, since the church could not be responsible for the actual shedding of blood. The Inquisition—which began in some locales in the mid 1100s and continued in some places (Spain, for instance) into the 1800s—might be chief among those "very bad things" that result from too close a marriage of church and state.

Waldo himself disappeared sometime after 1184, when the pope declared the Waldensians heretics instead of schismatics. (Okay, *now* you can say it. Where's . . . ?) The Waldensians, however, persisted in individual villages hidden in various valleys of eastern Europe until the Reformation, when they generally merged themselves with the newer Protestant groups.

The High Middle Ages was obviously a time of great religious ferment, when any new groups (even those like the Franciscans and Dominicans) might suddenly be deemed to be schismatic (divisive influences) or even heretical. Maybe that makes the actions of Aquinas's family more understandable?

AQUINAS SET FREE

Their pleas and protests, however, fell on deaf ears. Aquinas had made up his mind. When the Dominicans appealed his case to both the pope and the emperor, his brothers released him, and Aquinas was free to follow his vocation. His supervisors had already recognized his brilliance, and they secured for him the greatest education available. He eventually studied with Albertus Magnus (Albert the Great), believed to be the sharpest mind in the Christian world. Thomas was big—almost hulking—with a large face and a tendency to hold his tongue until he was certain of what he wanted to say. His classmates called him the "dumb ox." Appearances can certainly be deceiving.

THE BRILLIANT DOCTOR

Aquinas remained with Albertus Magnus when he shifted schools between Cologne and Paris. He watched as his mentor debated the "new ideas" of the day—ideas that were actually extremely old. The Muslims had rediscovered Aristotle, and a Muslim scholar named Averroes was provoking questions among all the Christian scholars in Europe by citing his own interpretations of the ancient philosopher. Thomas was certain that Aristotle could be harmonized with the church's teachings, and he spent the rest of his life proving that.

While teaching the primary theological book of the time (Peter Lombard's *Sentences*), Thomas determined that he wanted to clear away the theological confusion he saw in his students. He began writing his *Summa Theologiae*, beginning with his famous Five Ways of proving God's existence by reasoning. He did not question at all the need for God's revelation of himself through Scripture. He did, however, make an extremely well-reasoned defense of belief in God.

THE *SUMMA THEOLOGIAE*

The *Summa Theologiae* is an extremely long work — about 1,500 pages of very small print in the GREAT BOOKS edition — but it is also incredibly brilliant. Aquinas asks a series of questions and then responds to each from the viewpoints of various thinkers. He applies the observations of "The Philosopher" (by which he means Aristotle) to most of these questions. He incorporates responses from Scripture along with the comments of the church fathers, especially Augustine. Then he sums up his own thinking on the issue, generally in such a powerfully reasonable way that any opponent is blown out of the debate.

He wrote this systematically, beginning with the nature of God. His framework for dealing systematically with theology has been the template for other theologians ever since. Not everyone agreed with everything he said — John Duns Scotus and William of Ockham, for example, criticized him for not acknowledging that reason and revelation often contradict each other — but no one had ever done such a thorough job of seeking to deal with every question about the nature of God, Christ, angels, and so on.

How *does* reason relate to faith? It's one of our primary themes because it has been a critical point of debate since the beginning of the church. Various wonderful believers have apparently disagreed through Christian history, much as it might appear from this chapter that Francis and Thomas would have disagreed. But did they?

People are different. They see things in different ways and have different experiences, and it is upon our experiences that we base our solutions to the problems we face. People express those differences with differing sequences of words.

Thomas felt pressed to respond to the challenge of Muslim intellectualism and to prove Christian thought superior. If that meant reshaping Aristotelian thought into Christian form, that was what he needed to do. Francis saw people—hurting, confused people—and he loved them. In his dealings with the poor, he had no use for intellectual reasoning. In his dealings with the educated, Aquinas could not afford to be *without* it. Both men contributed enormously to the church, and continue to do so. In that sense—their emphasis upon the importance of Christ and his church—they didn't disagree at all.

Dominic passed through a part of France where he saw things that appalled him: people believing heresy, people preaching to others without benefit of theological study, using the common language of the people. This so challenged his personal understanding of God that he was willing to borrow the heretics' common-language-preaching idea to try to persuade them to return to the church. Not everybody agreed with his methods, just as not everyone today agrees with churches that use rock music to try to reach a younger generation. The key in both cases, however, was loyalty to that same belief both Francis and Aquinas clung to—belief in Christ and his church.

It's even possible to defend some of the things Innocent III did—the Fourth Crusade that resulted in the sack of Constantinople, the crusade against the French heretics—on this same ground: He did it for Christ and his church. But on those same grounds you can defend both Waldo and the Inquisition, can't you?

This is why it's important to think for yourself about church history. Somewhere between "Only my way is true!" and "Any way is true!" — neither of which can be true — there is the truth. And it is always attacked from both of these poles. When you determine for yourself what you believe to be true, just expect that you will be attacked for it. Francis was. Aquinas was. And the question that is at the heart of this issue is simply, "On what authority do you base *your* understanding of truth?"

One knock on Aquinas is that his carefully reasoned theology was based not only upon Scripture but on the (not necessarily inspired) views of Aristotle, the church fathers, and the traditions of the Roman Catholic Church. The result was at times carefully reasoned speculations that may or may not have real basis in God's revelation. What he said about angels, for example, may not be true at all.

Aquinas was a faithful, fervent, brilliant scholar throughout his life. An interesting closing note regarding Aquinas is this: His *Summa Theologiae* was never finished — not by him, anyway. He was sometimes given to religious ecstasies, and one day he came out of worship saying he was putting down his pen. When his assistant asked him why, he said: "I've seen things so wonderful that all that I have written seems like nothing." Clearly this was a man of faith, one who harnessed the style of reason of his day to *explain* that faith, not to replace it.

A later pope declared that anyone who questioned Aquinas's writings would be considered outside the faith of the Roman Catholic Church. I doubt if Thomas would ever have made such a statement. He was too committed to reforming the *quest* for truth to have suggested that he had arrived at it.

Is there a right way to know God? Francis, Dominic, and Aquinas were different people whose minds worked in different ways, but they all knew God by faith. Reason is critical to faith—we cannot even understand the concept without our reason. Both are important. But, as Scripture says, "Without faith it is impossible to please Him" (Hebrews 11:6).

What do these great souls of the past have to say to our themes?

People Like Us

It may be difficult to see Francis, Dominic, or Aquinas as people like us—but they were. Each had his quirks, obsessions, and failures. Francis had been a fun-loving slacker as a kid—maybe he still was one when he turned his order over to the organizers? Did the institutionalizing of the Franciscan order alter his life's work? Could he have bent it back toward the simplicity he began with if he'd not pulled back from its leadership?

Dominic was absolutely certain of the truth of his own beliefs, but was willing to try innovative ways to make those truths clear to those who disagreed. I sure wouldn't fault him there, but did his personal imprint on the order that bears his name somehow uniquely suit the Dominicans to be the chief administrators of the Inquisition?

Aquinas was brilliant, but did that brilliance cause him to succumb to the belief that a well-reasoned argument is more important than a simply stated principle of Scripture? Did he come near to repudiating that view at the close of his life?

If you read these people's works, you can see their personalities come alive. And while I can't think of anyone I consider to have been more like Jesus than Francis, he wasn't Jesus. He was a man. (Doesn't that mean that we could each be more like Jesus if we really tried?)

The Body of Christ and the Human Institution

Much of this chapter has dealt with reformers—reformers within the Roman Catholic Church, but reformers nevertheless. The reason they made an impact is simple: They changed the human institution, and those changes were in the direction (for the most part) of bringing the church back toward being the body of Christ. The institutional church was clearly broken, and these saints struggled to work in concert with the Holy Spirit to fix it. The sad thing is how quickly these fresh new orders and writings became institutionalized themselves. (This happened in the Reformation too, and it happens today.)

Faith Versus Reason

These were men of great personal faith. It motivated their pursuit of the truth and of obedience to Christ. They worked at that in different ways: Francis distrusted education and reason, feeling too much education would interfere with service; Dominic wanted a mix of these elements, depending on the excellence of education and effective apologetic preaching to influence those whose faith, he believed, had been misplaced; Aquinas expressed his faith throughout his life with a near absolute commitment to reason.

Perhaps I personally respond most to Francis because the faith he expressed is timeless, while the reason of the time was subject to the style of thinking of the time. I say that as an academic, trying as best I can to teach and write effectively, apologetically, and reasonably—at least in the reason of *our* time. Styles of reasoning and the certainties of science are much like fashion—they change with the seasons. Reason must in every generation remain a servant to faith, not the other way around.

Church + State = Very Bad Things

The Inquisition. Need I say more? I've read a modern semijus-tification for the Inquisition, and I can only respond that it still looks like the Holocaust. I can understand it in its historical context. That I have to be associated with it as a Christian is humiliating. Along with the Crusades, the Inquisition is the historical reality that proves this rule: The church plus the state equals very bad things. *Any* inquisition, be it the ethnic cleansing of Serbia, or the tit-for-tat murders of Shiites and Sunnis in Iraq, or our own American witch trials in Salem, is a very bad thing. It is institutionalized evil, despite its rationalized morality.

Didn't Satan offer Jesus control of the kingdoms of the world if Jesus would only bow down and serve him? Political religion almost always leads to bowing down to Satan. We need to make certain that in our pursuit of the faith we don't become inquisitors ourselves.

What About Missions?

Missions motivated both Francis and Dominic. Francis sent his Friars Minor on missions, and despite his poor health he became a missionary himself. From the Franciscans and Dominicans (and one other group we'll discuss in a couple of chapters—the Jesuits) came some of the greatest missionaries in church history. During this period of spiritual ferment and religious horror, this truth indicates Christ's continued presence in his body. People gave their lives to go and tell. Missionary methods like the Crusades and the Inquisition were disastrous and should never be repeated, and Francis's mission to the Muslims ultimately bore little fruit, but some of the groundwork for later missions was laid.

Ethics Optional?

The ethical failure of the institutional church became overwhelmingly apparent during this period. The sin and self-indulgence of some leaders made reformation critical — and reformation began within the church. But the fact that the reformations didn't go to the top of the leadership chain or to the heart of the traditions meant that more reformation was inevitable.

The next round of reforms, which changed the church forever, began in the cell of an Augustinian monk who couldn't find peace with what he had been taught. Martin Luther had questions. Questions couldn't be tolerated. Think: train wreck.

WANT TO KNOW MORE?

There is perhaps more written about Francis than any other saint. He lived in an age of written records, and many people commented on him. In addition, he wrote things himself, especially poems and hymns. There are also many excellent resources about Dominic and Aquinas. One source is the websites of the Franciscan and Dominican orders. The Catholic Encyclopedia has wonderful articles on each of these, and it is free online.

Faith Alone!
Scripture Alone!
Luther — Alone?

MARTIN LUTHER

So Martin Luther is sitting in his office, or study, or cell, or wherever, and he's thinking about people heading across the border to buy indulgences from a Dominican monk named Johann Tetzel. He's heard that Tetzel says, "Whenever a coin in the coffer rings, a soul from purgatory springs!" It's a good line, and people—some of Luther's people—are tossing in coins to get their relatives out of spiritual jail. Martin is fuming because he used to be like these people—terrified of offending God, certain that millions of years of punishment in purgatory awaited him, obsessed with fears of devils and doom. He'd pushed through all of that to a new understanding of the Bible's authority and its revelation of a loving God. He'd come to a new realization of the central place of faith and grace in salvation. Through reading the works of the patron saint of his Augustinian order (that would be Augustine, of course), he'd come to a belief in the certainty of God's love.

Having been a relentless and anxious perfectionist about his spiritual performance, Luther *needed* that certainty.

And now this Tetzel fellow, who'd been forbidden to sell his indulgences in Wittenberg, was standing outside the border selling heaven to poor people who didn't realize that they already *had* it, taking money from them they couldn't afford to spend, all for the sake of a pope who wanted money to build a beautiful church. I'm guessing that Martin was getting redder and redder in the face as he thought about this (he was an overweight fellow who could get really stirred up when he believed something passionately).

So he wrote out ninety-five things (history calls them *theses*) that he wanted to debate publicly, and he nailed them to the door of the castle church. The date was October 31, 1517. The Protestant Reformation had begun.

Well, not really. In fact, the spirit of reformation had been growing for a long time. Francis, Dominic, Aquinas, and others had been reforming the church from within. Others who had been termed schismatics or heretics had struggled for reform and been burned for it or forced into hiding. John Wycliffe had translated the Bible into English, allowing people to read for themselves the difference between what the Scriptures said and what the church tradition had become. The Czech reformer Jan Hus had attended the Council of Constance to defend his views. Although he went there with a safe-conduct pass from the emperor, he was burned at the stake before he had a chance to share his perspective. But Martin Luther and his movement survived because of politics, sociological changes, and technology. He didn't intend to leave the church. He wanted to reform it, not start a revolution. But things took off, and that's why this date in history has become so important.

Europe was politically ready for change because the struggle between the secular rulers and the popes—and between one king and another—had reached a crisis point. Yes, there were moral problems in the church, but there had been for centuries—really since the beginning. But the emperor of the Holy Roman Empire and the kings of emerging nations found the pope's political involvement in their affairs more and more frustrating. Why, these kings believed, should someone in Rome challenge their divine right to rule?

Also, Europe's sociology was changing with the advance of trade, education, and technology, and the emerging middle class of merchants and town leaders wanted more independence. With more education, Europeans thought more and more for themselves. Universities started in Aquinas's day were flourishing. For the first time, the Greek New Testament was widely available to educated laypeople. Erasmus was commenting on the Scriptures and writing about humanism.

But one of the most critical changes that impacted this time was technological: Gutenberg had invented moveable type. The Bible could now be printed rather than copied by hand, which made it cheap enough for middle-class people to buy. And Luther's Ninety-Five Theses were also printed, so within weeks his complaint circulated not just around his town but all over Europe. Like the Internet in our day, the printing press was a mass communications device that made widespread grassroots conversation and demand for reform possible.

With princes chafing against the pope's political power and technology spreading new ideas to the masses, the Protestant Reformation (note the capital letters) took off. Church leaders couldn't burn books fast enough to stop it. But in 1517, they still believed they could, and Martin Luther's protest wasn't immediately regarded as terribly threatening. Bad mistake.

LUTHER'S FEAR

There was a time when more books had been published about Martin Luther than anyone in history except Jesus. I think Luther has surely now been passed by another German named Adolf, although I may be wrong. But there remain an enormous number of sources that relate the facts of Luther's life.

MARTIN LUTHER
1483–1546

Luther was a German monk who became a professor, a theologian, and a religious celebrity who influenced Western Christianity enormously and helped launch the Protestant Reformation. His positions on *sola scriptura* (Scripture alone is the authority) and *sola fide* (faith alone is the requirement for salvation) became the key watchwords of the Reformed churches that emerged in Europe.

When charged with heresy and threatened with death, he was "kidnapped" by his own supporters and hidden, and he remained protected for the rest of his life, despite being publicly condemned by the pope. His translation of the Bible into German affected not only the German church (and German language) but also the English translation that has been called the King James Version. He elevated preaching and hymn singing in his personal ministry, establishing these as the central activities of Protestant worship.

Luther was born into the family of a successful German miner, so he experienced a relatively privileged childhood. But the Germany he grew up in was a superstitious place, and the Roman Catholic doctrine he was taught made God frightening to him. The importance—and terror—of purgatory made him particularly sensitive to supernatural events, and the only real place of refuge from these fears was the monastery. He was fulfilling his father's wishes and training to be a lawyer when he was almost struck by lightning. He swore he'd enter a monastery if God preserved him, and he followed up that promise by becoming an Augustinian.

His father was furious—yet another instance of father-son friction concerning a spiritual call—but Luther remained in the monastery anyway. His colleagues saw him as a holier-than-thou superspiritual irritant. He confessed everything he could think of, hoping to soothe his fears of God. It didn't work.

FACING AUGUSTINE

The Augustinian order had been drawn together from older groups at about the same time as the Dominicans and Franciscans were founded. Although not connected historically to Augustine, they followed his rule and dedicated themselves to his thought. Luther sank himself into study of Augustine, and this is part of the reason why Augustinian thought has had such continuing influence on Protestantism.

Luther was bothered, though, by Augustine's emphasis on predestination and irresistible grace. The picture of God this gave him was even more terrifying than the one he'd brought into the monastery. This God was bound by no rules except his own whim and could capriciously decide anyone's eternal life or death. Worse, this God had already decided people's eternal destiny since the foundation of the world! Luther wrote, "This appears iniquitous, cruel, and intolerable in God, by which very many have been offended in all ages. And who would not be? I was myself more than once driven to the very abyss of despair so that I wished I had never been created. Love God? I hated him!"

Luther confessed his sins at length—sometimes for six hours. His superior in the order, Johann von Staupitz, had a solution: He made Luther a professor at the new school in Wittenberg. But while teaching the Scriptures, Luther came to a new understanding of the power of the Bible and simple faith. He finally felt personal release. This insight caused him to reject the weighty tradition of winning salvation through good works and set him on his path of opposition to the church's teaching. The explosion point came when he finally spoke out against indulgences.

THE INDULGENCE CONTROVERSY

The idea of indulgences came from the view that saints of the past had built up more merit than they needed by their wonderful acts and that the church could apply this merit to the sins of others through indulgences. Innocent III had issued indulgences to crusaders willing to fight for God in the Holy Land. The practice then was extended to those who gave money to the church. Indulgences could be gained by making pilgrimages to various places to view the relics of the saints.

Wittenberg had many relics. They included a tear Jesus cried over Jerusalem, feathers from the wings of an angel, a twig from the burning bush, and one of Peter's thigh bones—one of at least five that Luther knew about. He determined the whole practice was a fraud. While the church he served—and that paid his salary—was in part supported by money gained from these relics, he could no longer remain silent. In 1516, he began to preach against the practice. When Johann Tetzel came selling indulgences for the coins of poor peasants, Luther exploded.

UNDER FIRE

The pope and the emperor were busy fighting the Turks, but the head of the Inquisition summoned Luther to Rome to face charges. He'd been to Rome before and had returned disgusted by the immorality he saw there — especially among the priests. It seemed the closer he got to the Holy City, the less seriously the priests took their own message. He refused to go. His prince, Frederick of Saxony, intervened on his behalf and got the trial shifted to Germany.

Luther met with Cardinal Cajetan at Augsberg but wouldn't recant. A former friend named Johann Eck challenged him to a debate in Leipzig, and for three weeks they argued about Luther's ideas. Eck felt he won the debate, for by his probing he got Luther to endorse the views of Jan Hus, the declared heretic who'd been burned a century before. Luther was saved from the same fate by the timely death of the Holy Roman Emperor.

The pope preferred that the next emperor be someone more manageable, the head of a small state like Frederick of Saxony. Frederick was Luther's prince, and Luther his star attraction, so the pope backed off. He even went so far as to revise the doctrine of indulgences, tightening up the way they were applied. Tetzel was put out of a job. But Luther continued his writings, and the frustrated pope finally issued a papal bull (a formal charge) saying that "a wild boar had been loosed in the vineyard." Luther was the boar.

When the document arrived, Luther burned it publicly. The new emperor, the powerful Charles V, whom the pope could *not* control, summoned Luther to Worms to answer the charges against him. He was given a promise of safe conduct, but he knew how that had worked out for Jan Hus. Still, he had the support of Frederick and also of moderate Catholics who had been influenced by Erasmus. Luther went.

THE DIET OF WORMS

He stood before the diet (that means the council—I know it looks bizarre in English) and took responsibility for his own writings. He was told to recant his views, and he asked for a night to think it over. The next day he made his famous response:

> Unless I am convicted by the Scriptures and plain reason — I do not accept the authority of popes and councils, for they have contradicted each other — my conscience is captive to the Word of God. I cannot and will not recant anything, for to go against conscience is neither right nor safe. Here I stand. I can do no other. God help me. Amen.

When he left Worms, he was kidnapped off the road and disappeared for nearly a year. In fact, he was taken to Wartburg Castle and kept there under protection at Frederick's command. It proved a good thing for Luther, because a month after the diet Charles V issued an edict declaring him a "manifest heretic" and forbidding any subject of the emperor to give him lodging, food, or drink. He was to be arrested on sight and turned over to the emperor. His books were banned, and even his friends were to be arrested. It was never enforced, but it stayed in effect for the rest of his life. Luther was an outlaw.

LUTHERANISM

While at Wartburg Castle, Luther wrote constantly. He got a lot done. But things in Wittenburg were falling apart. His protégé, Philipp Melanchthon, took charge, but he didn't have Luther's strength to handle the rebellion. Luther returned — still under the emperor's ban — and began to set up a new church. It was to be based on his two primary principles of *sole fide* and *sola scriptura.* There would be no priests, for Luther believed in the priesthood of the believers. By that he meant that no priest stood between the individual and Christ. Because there was no longer any need for priests or monasteries, those monasteries that followed Luther emptied — and Luther married one of the former nuns.

He moderated the theology of sacraments, too. The church held that through the Eucharist, which was the heart of the Mass, the bread and the cup literally turned into Christ's body and blood through transubstantiation. Luther denied that view, substituting the idea of consubstantiation, meaning that the bread and wine did not literally change, but that somehow Christ was still present in both. He didn't explain how, and this became the primary reason why the leaders of the Swiss reformation (see chapter 8 on John Calvin) didn't join the Lutherans in a single Protestant church. In place of the Eucharist, Luther elevated preaching as the central activity of worship. He also loved congregational singing, and he wrote and published a hymnbook. Two of his best known hymns are "A Mighty Fortress Is Our God" and "Away in a Manger."

And though this world, with devils filled, should threaten to undo
us,
We will not fear, for God has willed His truth to triumph through
us. . . .
Let goods and kindred go, this mortal life also;
The body they may kill: God's truth abideth still,
His kingdom is forever.

MARTIN LUTHER, "A MIGHTY FORTRESS IS OUR GOD"

LUTHER'S LOW POINTS

So then, the great reformer was practically perfect in every way, right? No. Just like the rest of the figures we've discussed, Luther had his flaws.

For many of the German peasants who had supported Luther and his rebellion at the beginning, the changes didn't go far enough. They wanted political changes as well as spiritual ones, and they revolted against their noble overlords. At first Luther was in agreement, but these revolts were led in several places by radical reformers—preachers who took the Scriptures as their justification for political reform and who sometimes stimulated followers to do terrible things. After peasants massacred the people of Weinsberg, Luther turned on them. He called on the princes to kill them all as if they were mad dogs.

Whether in response to him or on their own initiative, both Lutheran and Catholic princes went to work, killing one hundred thousand people. Luther then turned on the princes for their brutality, but the deed was done. Besides, while he had stood up to Rome itself, he wasn't in any position to stand up to the Lutheran princes who had supported his reformation. He sided with the existing authorities in northern Europe, and the Lutheran Church found safety and room to grow. But the issue was far from resolved—once the emperor finally defeated the Turks at the gates of Vienna, he turned his attention to putting down this Protestant rebellion. Religious wars were coming. Luther didn't live to see them, but did he sense that they were just around the corner?

Luther couldn't do much about the coming wars, but he might have thought more about missions. His view was that if God wanted to save the heathen, he was surely able to do so. Why would he need our help? To those who read the Great Commission and see the book of Acts as the report of a continuing missionary effort, this attitude seems—unscriptural. Does *sola scriptura* mean only those parts of the Scripture you like alone? Or does it mean that all Scripture is applicable? This issue was the problem the so-called radical reformers had with Martin Luther. He pointed everybody back to the Bible but not necessarily *all* of it.

Perhaps the biggest criticism of Luther has been of his blind spot concerning the Jews. To say that what he wrote about the Jewish race was anti-Semitic is an understatement. He said the rights of Jews should be limited, their money should be taken from them, their homes should be razed to the ground, and their schools and synagogues should be burned. That sounds a lot like the words of that *other* German that so many books have been written about—you know, Adolf? Hitler and the Nazis made much of the writings of Luther when they established the Third Reich. They did pretty much exactly what Martin Luther had suggested. How far do you have to go from

Luther's suggestions to arrive at the death camps?

We will all have things to answer for when we stand before the Judgment. But in large measure because of Martin Luther—and the timing of events around him—many of us can look forward to that Judgment with nowhere near the *dread* young Luther felt. We can read the Scriptures and interpret them for ourselves. We can see in the Bible God's love as well as his justice. We can respond with an understanding of the transforming power of faith alone.

So what does the life of this pivotal thinker say to our themes?

People Like Us

Was Martin Luther a person like us? The Jews certainly think so. But he was also a courageous person to be so relatively insignificant and take such a stand before the Holy Roman Emperor and the pope. He studied until he understood. He taught what he believed God had showed him. He held fast to his faith in the face of overwhelming odds. He had significant flaws, but he was a brave man.

The Body of Christ and the Human Institution

All of Luther's early criticisms of the church really came down to this question: Was the church being what God intended? Luther said No!—but he didn't intend to split it. He just wanted to see it return to the faith of the Bible, as have many others before and since. It still sounds like a good idea.

Faith Versus Reason

Luther argued that justification was by faith alone. Where do you think he would come down on the tension between faith and reason? Actually, he was very much a believer in reason as well as faith. He was a scholar and a teacher who based many of his ideas on a *reasonable* interpretation of Scripture. His reason wouldn't permit him to ignore the indulgence question. He argued for a healthy balance of both — with faith taking the lead.

Church + State = Very Bad Things

This seems obvious from the chapter you've just read. But the massacre of the peasants by the princes reminds us that the church-state problem doesn't apply just to the Roman Catholic Church or to a state in relationship with a pope. Luther tied the salaries of Lutheran pastors to the German state to cut them away from the financial control of Rome. So when the Nazis took over the German government, they controlled the church leaders of Germany with this same apparatus. There really is a lot of value in the radical reformation idea of the separation of church and state, allowing the church to influence the state but allowing neither one to control the other.

What About Missions?

The great reformers' faulty theology of missions led to a three-hundred-year failure to take the Great Commission seriously. This period of Protestant history is sometimes termed "the great omission." The Reformation didn't misplace missions any more than the Catholic Church did during this period — it just didn't rediscover missions along with other biblical truths.

Ethics Optional?

It was the character — the ethos — of the church and its leaders that stirred Luther to react as he did. He saw the church's failures clearly and attacked them courageously. He didn't see his own ethical failures nearly as clearly. Few of us do. That such blind spots could hinder such a great leader should prompt us all to ask others to help us see our own blind spots.

WANT TO KNOW MORE?

There are literally millions of references to Luther on the Internet. But if you want to read some good books, you might look up Roland H. Bainton's *Here I Stand* (Nashville: Abingdon Press, 1950) or Mike Fearon's *Martin Luther*, part of Bethany House's MEN OF FAITH series. There are also many translations of Luther's works.

It's the Will of God!

CALVIN AND LOYOLA

Guillaume Farel had fomented reformation/rebellion against the Catholic Church all over Switzerland and had been sent to the city of Geneva to do the same. He was really good at starting debate but not great at administration. When he heard that a young man named John Calvin was spending the night in the city, he trapped Calvin in his room. "It's God's will for you to stay!" he thundered at the young scholar, who had already made a name for himself by writing an inflammatory letter to the king of France. Poor John Calvin. He was only passing through town. But if it was God's will for him to stay in Geneva, he had to stay, right?

JOHN CALVIN (JEAN CAUVIN)
1509–1564

A French lawyer converted to Reformation views in 1532, Calvin became the leader of the second generation of the Reformation in Europe. Persecuted for his faith, he fled Paris and in 1534 was enlisted to lead the reform of the church in Geneva,

Switzerland. Apart from four years spent in Austria, Calvin essentially governed Geneva until his death. The laws he established and strictly enforced would be viewed today as intrusions into personal freedoms. He is best known for writing *Institutes of the Christian Religion*, and his name is forever linked with the doctrine of the absolute sovereignty of God and predestination (see "TULIP" on pages 167-168). Calvin's influence is seen throughout Protestantism but especially in Presbyterian, Dutch Reformed, and Baptist churches.

Have you ever had anybody manipulate you with the old "It's God's will!" line? I have. I was once an administrator in a school with another man, who shared an office wall with me. We were at the same level on the flowchart, but he was a generation older than I and had taught my older brother, so I guess he believed I was still a student. Whenever I did something that displeased him, he would take me out to lunch and tell me—in these words—"That's not what *God* told *me*!" I don't know if he ever figured out that feeding me lunch every time he got angry was positive reinforcement for my frustrating behavior. What it did solidify in me was how easily some can make God the author of whatever they want to see happen. It makes me want to ask, "How do you know?"

If we asked John Calvin, "How do you know?" we'd doubtless get the response, "It's in the Bible!" As we saw with Luther, the Reformation was all about people saying God's will is revealed in Scripture, not in the traditions of the church or the writings of the ancient fathers. The thing is, during the 1500s, if you said, "God's will is *this*," when the powers-that-be said, "God's will is *that*," they'd likely cut off your head or burn you at the stake. Calvin was on the road through Geneva because there was a stake with his name on it, and, all things considered, he was a lawyer, not a martyr. Farel was asking him to plant himself in a particular place and raise his targeted head high. He didn't want to. But Farel pushed the right button. It was "God's will." Calvin proceeded to write, preach, and pressure the leaders of Geneva to adopt his version of "God's will," to which, it must be said, many Christians subscribe today.

THE ROAD TO GENEVA

Calvin was a very moral boy growing up in his father's house in Noyon, France. His father was a lawyer for the priests in that city, and John was marked early for the priesthood. But his father and the priests apparently didn't agree on God's will, and Dad sent John to study law instead. This he did, beginning university in Paris at the age of fourteen. He loved the classics, Latin, and Greek, and self-published his first book on the secular Roman Seneca's *De Clementia* (On Clemency).

It's interesting that the twenty-two-year-old scholar should focus his attention on a letter to Emperor Nero about the necessity of showing clemency (mercy, restraint) to his subjects. In his later life Calvin didn't show much clemency to those who ran afoul of *his* understanding of God's law. There was no religious content in his early book, however. Then in 1532 or 1533, Calvin changed. The good little Catholic boy became a Protestant outlaw.

Why? How? We don't know. He didn't say enough about his experience for us to know exactly what happened. But this much is clear: Calvin didn't choose God—God chose Calvin. This is clearly how he felt, and in this was the seed of his emphasis on "election." God does with us what God wants to do with us.

How can any of us know the nature of another person's relationship to God in Christ Jesus? Only by their fruits, the Bible says. So what were the fruits of Calvin's conversion? He had long been receiving income from a church position for which he wasn't performing the duties—a kind of "scholarship" arranged by his father. He resigned this.

He began to meet in secret with groups in Paris who longed to see the church reformed. He became a leader among them. He *may* have ghostwritten a sermon for Nicolas Cop, the young rector of the university, which praised the supposedly Lutheran doctrine of salvation by grace through faith. Whether Calvin wrote it, helped write it, or had nothing to do with it, he was rumored to be connected with the heretical sermon. Cop was arrested, and Calvin almost was. Friends in his house delayed the police and let him down from the window on bed sheets, and he left Paris dressed as a vinedresser with a hoe over his shoulder.

He spent the next few months sneaking in and out of Paris like a spiritual terrorist, meeting with Protestant groups who were later discovered—and burned. It was a harsh time. But Calvin was faithful to what he saw as God's will. (Eventually that would lead him to become a burner rather than a burnee. One day Calvin waited in Paris to meet with another Reformation firebrand, a man named Michael Servetus. Servetus didn't show up that day, but when he showed up in Geneva years later, Calvin played a role in burning *him*.)

From the relative safety of Switzerland, Calvin wrote a letter to the king of France. In it he spelled out the theology that eventually became *Institutes of the Christian Religion*. Based on his legal understanding of reasonable, logical thinking and (we guess) upon his personal experience with God's election, Calvin's mind was made up. He was certain that God was absolutely sovereign in all things, including the question of who would be saved. God had predestined the elect for salvation, and because he had determined it to be so, it would be.

While this doctrine offended Luther, Calvin embraced it with a legal-minded certainty. This letter brought him fame among the Reformers—and to Guillaume Farel's attention. When Calvin tried to go to Austria, he found the road blocked by a war between the king of France and the Holy Roman Emperor. Taking the long road around led him through Geneva, and Farel learned he was spending the night in town. Calvin had already made himself clear on what he believed to be God's will. Now Farel pinned him like an insect under that same heavenly tack. Calvin stayed.

THEOLOGY WITH EMPHASIS ON THE "LOGY"

There are several paintings of Calvin. He doesn't look happy. But the people of Geneva weren't all that happy either. Together, Calvin and Farel pressured, cajoled, prompted, and shamed the Geneva city council into legislating morality into all of Genevan life. They had grown up in a society where the church and the state walked hand-in-hand—just not very comfortably—and they believed that the purpose of the state was to enforce God's law on its citizens. They wrote a confession of faith for Geneva that gave "ministers of the word" the responsibility to excommunicate—and banish—Genevans who didn't accept it or live up to it. These included idolaters, blasphemers, murderers, thieves, fornicators, false witnesses, seditious people, quarrelers, slanderers, batterers, drunkards, and wasters of goods. Calvin was a legal scholar. Could such a mind be expected to provide anything other than a legalistic system for abiding by God's will?

There was a great spiritual revival in Geneva, and people committed themselves to God with apparent sincerity. But people forget, sometimes, what they commit themselves to believe. For eighteen months "the preachers" (that's what all of Geneva called them) haunted the councils of Geneva, prodding the city fathers to enforce the laws of morality. Calvin was apparently the type of person you either loved or hated, probably because he was certain of what he believed and was courageous enough to say it. He and Farel made enemies in the city—powerful enemies.

Eventually they were driven out, and it appears that the young Calvin (he was only twenty-eight by this time) felt greatly relieved. He went to Austria and became the pastor of a church full of French refugees. There he developed his own style of what church should be. After a rather comical search for a marriage partner that kept running into dead ends, he found a wife in his congregation. For four years he seems to have been very happy—until Geneva came calling again. The city fathers wanted him back, and they committed to follow Christ if he would be their spiritual leader. Once again he had to face that "call of God" thing. With many tears, he moved his wife to a house provided for him by the city and began to lead.

FIRST (NON)CITIZEN OF GENEVA

The result of Calvin's leadership from the pulpit was thoroughgoing reform, which has echoed with both positive and negative results into our own generation. Three hundred years earlier, another reformer had seen the same need for the church to change, but St. Francis had been a lover not a lawyer. You may remember that Francis felt so incapable of setting up a system of rules for the Franciscans that he had turned the task over to others. Calvin's strengths and weaknesses were almost the polar opposite.

Many Christians in the four hundred years since Calvin have been blessed by his honest, urgent teaching. But others feel that the God whom Calvin presents to us is less approachable than the Jesus of the Scriptures. He was a child of his age in this. At university he had read Erasmus, the humanist scholar whose ideas had fueled the Reformation. Calvin's dependence on reason required that all aspects of the Scripture be harmonized into one logical system, and that required some interpretive decisions. Some of these had already been made for him by Augustine. Calvin wrote a logical explanation of God that kept growing in length, but not changing in thought, until the end of his life. It is all very logical. But is it an accurate depiction of the interactions between God, Christ Jesus, the church, and the individual Christian? Are there mysteries in God that are beyond our understanding (and systematizing) — mysteries into which even angels long to look? In stressing logic and obedience, does Calvin underrate love and grace?

TULIP

Calvin's theology has been summed up with the acronym TULIP. Humankind is Totally depraved and can play no part in salvation. Those whom God chose to be the elect receive his unmerited favor, which has nothing to do with their actions. This is Unconditional election. God is not being arbitrary in this because all have sinned and deserve death. God is well within his rights as

God to choose to save whomever he will. Jesus died for the elect alone — not for everybody. If he'd died for all people, then all people would be saved — and they're not. There was, therefore, only Limited atonement on the cross. Because God elects whomever he will, those who are chosen have no personal choice in the matter — this is called Irresistible grace. Because salvation is an act of God and not in any way dependent on human action, nothing the elect person does can cause him to lose his salvation. This is the Perseverance of the saints.

Calvin held no public office. He wasn't even a citizen of Geneva until the council made him one late in life. Still, in effect, he governed the city. There was constant opposition, but he mostly won the battles. The city was changed. Although he was never a healthy man, he preached or taught every day, and he wrote. Other Reformation leaders sought his counsel, so he kept up a steady stream of correspondence with people all over Europe.

He became a friend of Luther's right-hand man, Melanchthon, but Calvin and Luther could never see eye-to-eye on the nature of Christ's presence in Communion, so their churches never united. Their temperaments were very different, as was the way they applied Scripture: For Luther, church traditions that weren't forbidden by Scripture could be continued. For Calvin, if a practice wasn't prescribed in the Bible, you didn't do it. On the question of the relation of faith to reason, Luther came down heavily on the side of faith. Calvin came down on the side of reason.

Calvin did his job. He worked tirelessly as one of the pastors of the city, doing all the things pastors still do and providing a model for pastors everywhere. He visited the sick until the Black Plague came to Geneva and the city fathers prevented him. He worked even though he was often ill and suffered from a chronic headache. His son died as a baby. His wife died several years later, probably of tuberculosis. She was on her deathbed when he had to run out for an appointment at 6:00 p.m., but he managed to make it back in time for her actual death around 7:30. Was this a personal tragedy? Certainly. As he put it, he had been deprived of his best companion. But he apparently didn't dwell on it. You may have heard about the Protestant work ethic. This is its source. There was work to be done.

And enemies of God's will to contend against. Since Calvin saw the state as a tool to help people maintain excellence in Christian living, he saw no problem in using the city laws to punish those who failed to live up to his standards. If you want to know where the Puritan heritage in America came from, look no further than Calvin's Geneva. Many of the old families of the city were unhappy with the strictures the preachers enforced through the city council. They felt invaded by outsiders and struggled to get their old life back. This party, the Libertines, conspired against Calvin in various ways. The best known was through their support of that Spaniard named Servetus, who had stood up Calvin in Paris years before.

CALVIN VERSUS SERVETUS

Servetus didn't believe in the Trinity, and he published a book saying so. The Roman Catholic Church banned it and branded Servetus a heretic. When Calvin went on to Geneva and declared himself publicly for a renewed church, Servetus disappeared. He hid in the French city of Lyon, taking an assumed name and working as a physician. He was a stalwart member of the local Catholic congregation, even though he didn't believe in Catholicism. He did, however, write letters to Calvin, debating him at many points.

Calvin responded in many exchanges. Even though he found Servetus's beliefs heretical, he didn't turn him in to the Catholic authorities. Still, when Servetus was discovered and arrested, it was indirectly through this contact between them. Servetus escaped from prison. The Catholics tried him for heresy anyway and found him guilty, then burned him in effigy. Servetus escaped from France and passed through Geneva. Exactly why isn't known, but Calvin recognized him and had him arrested.

The trial would certainly be featured on Court TV today. Servetus—supported by the Libertines—charged Calvin with making God ultimately responsible for sin. That's one of the major knocks still thrown at Calvinism. That is, if an all-sovereign God permits people to sin and then damns them to hell for it, isn't God and not the sinner responsible for sin? Servetus said Geneva should strip Calvin of his possessions and give them to him, then have them switch roles—Calvin in jail and Servetus in the pulpit. It appears that Servetus foolishly thought he was going to win.

The city fathers petitioned other Reformation cities for opinions on what to do with Servetus, and the responses were in effect unanimous: burn him as a heretic. The city council sentenced Servetus to burn at the stake. Calvin protested. Not against the death sentence—he just thought it would be more humane to kill Servetus with a sword.

Of course, that was the spirit of the time: People were being killed on all sides for their faith. Even so, I can't see Francis doing this. I can't see Paul doing this. Being burned *for* his faith, yes. But even in that Paul gave a caveat: "Though I give my body to be burned, but have not love, it profits me nothing" (1 Corinthians 13:3). I can't see Paul burning anyone else for his beliefs—nor even (humanely) running him through with a sword. Somewhere in the absolute certainties of throwing "It's God's will!" around, agape love tends to get scorched. What's left? Legalism, with an eye out for those who speak and write heretically, marking them for later burning.

Servetus burned. Farel went to watch. Calvin didn't. Perhaps he was too tender-hearted to stand it. Or perhaps burning heretics had become so commonplace that "if you've seen one burn, you've seen them all." After all, by 1546—seven years *before* Servetus was burned—fifty-eight people had been executed in Geneva for failing to live up to Calvin's understanding of God's standards. And in the days to come many, many, *many* others would perish across Europe—all in Jesus' name.

CALVINOCRACY?

One of the fearful things about those who trumpet "It's God's will!" is that those who join up with them feel no freedom to question their choices later—even if they come to feel a certain something is not God's will at all. Instead, the demand for conformity grows stronger until the church falls back into the control of a few loud men. The Reformation reformed the institutional church into—more institutional churches.

What shall we say, then? The Reformation was wonderful! Just not wonderful enough. And it got sidetracked.

BELIEVE IT IS WHITE

In his certainty about God's will, Calvin was not far different from another spiritual general of the time—a one-legged former warrior named Ignatius Loyola. They had, in fact, been students at the University of Paris at the same time—although there is no record that they ever met. And while Calvin was moving away from the Roman Church, Loyola used his time at university to enlist supporters of his *Spiritual Exercises* who would commit themselves wholeheartedly to the pope. So fervent was his defense of the Roman Church that he taught his followers, "Though it looks black to you, if the church says it is white, believe it is white."

Loyola's followers eventually banded themselves into a new Catholic order that was as missionary minded as the Franciscans and as committed to education as the Dominicans. They were willing to use whatever means necessary to destroy the "cancer" of the Reformation. They were known contemptuously by their critics as Jesuits, because they called themselves the Society of Jesus. Eventually they came to wear that name proudly. They were the shock troops of the Counter-Reformation, the Catholic reaction to the Protestant revolt. And if Calvin was the leading general of the Protestant cause, Loyala was his counterpart. The role fit his personality.

INIGO LOPEZ DE LOYOLA
1491–1556

Born in Spain to a wealthy family, Ignatius (he changed his name from Inigo after his conversion) began his professional life as a soldier. Wounded in battle and beyond all hope of returning to war, he dedicated himself instead to be a warrior for Jesus Christ and the Roman Catholic Church. Beset by many troubles in his life, he valiantly struggled to gain the education that would allow him to preach, all the time perfecting his masterwork, *The Spiritual*

Exercises. He became the founder and first superior general of the Society of Jesus, a religious order modeled on a military cadre and sworn to direct service to the pope. His followers, called Jesuits, have been some of the foremost Catholic missionaries of history, and have been loved and hated by many.

LIKE FRANCIS?

Loyola was a warrior. Born into a noble family in Spain, he was, like Francis, a younger child in a large family. And like Calvin, he was set aside early to be a member of the clergy, but he showed little inclination that way. As a boy, he never wore the robes of a cleric nor had his hair tonsured (that's the little bald spot shaved on the top of a priest's head at that time). Instead he dressed in finery, like Francis, and practiced the art of war.

The cocky young Loyola once had to be restrained from killing a man in the street for bumping into him. Like Francis, Loyola experienced an early tragedy in battle that changed his life. But while both Francis and Loyola charismatically attracted followers to them, Francis led from the heart, while Loyola led from the gut. In battle against the French, Loyola urged his troops to never surrender — until his legs got shot out from under him by a cannonball. Half of one shin was torn away, and the other leg was broken. The fortress he was defending fell, but the French were so impressed with his bravery that they carried him back to his home. There his leg was set — wrongly — then rebroken and set again — again wrongly (a stump of bone actually was projecting out of his leg!).

Due only to his vanity (as he said later), he had the bone

broken and set again, although the pain was terrible. During his long convalescence, he asked that books on knights and chivalry be brought to him, but there were none in the castle. Instead he read the Bible and the lives of the saints, and began to compete in his mind against these holy men who had gone before him. When he was able to walk again, his brother tried to dissuade him from doing anything rash—all he talked about now were spiritual things—but his mind was set. He was going to give his life to God.

His first task was to confess everything he could think of that he had ever done, during which—much like Luther—he wore out his confessor. Like Francis, he prayed alone in a chapel after a lengthy fast and saw a vision. He saw the virgin Mary holding the baby Jesus, and he was filled with both a loathing for his past sins and a longing to serve the church as a soldier of Christ. He hung up his sword and armor on Mary's statue. Like Francis, he gave away his rich clothes, put on a rough robe, and walked out to start a new life. But Ignatius Loyola was no Francis of Assisi. He was a fighter, not a lover. He left that imprint upon the Society of Jesus.

LOYOLA'S MILITARY CORPS

Loyola followed many of the same paths Francis did, including making his own trip to the Holy Land. There the Franciscans turned him away. As he gained his education, he preached his beliefs fervently, and the Dominican inquisitors arrested him. The Inquisition was concerned about his preaching without proper preparation, so he got that preparation. Three groups of disciples attached themselves to him as he earned the credentials that would allow him to speak. The first two groups fell away because the life was too hard. The third group, who joined him while he studied at the University of Paris, became the core of the Jesuits.

He organized the order along military lines—even calling it a military order. He had a hard time getting papal approval and initially was told the order would be limited to sixty members. But as the Society of Jesus proved to the popes its worth in solving spiritual (and political) problems swiftly and efficiently, this cap was lifted and the order expanded.

As Francis had before him, Loyola divided up his followers and sent them to various parts of the world. This was the period of Spanish expansion in the Americas, and Jesuits (or Franciscans, or Dominicans, or Augustinians) traveled with every conquistador, spreading the gospel as a part of the colonial reshaping of the world.

Not all of these missionaries believed in forcing baptism with the sword—some, in fact, represented the best Christian tradition of seeking to win people through education and preaching. Among these was Francis Xavier, one of those who first joined Loyola in Paris. Xavier went first to Goa, off the coast of India, then to India itself, then to Southeast Asia, and finally to Japan. He won many in Japan to Christ, establishing a church of about one hundred thousand before trying to move into China. He failed in this, dying as he waited to get into that vast empire, but he was followed eventually by Matteo Ricci.

Ricci adapted the essence of the gospel to the cultural context of the people. He learned Chinese, dressed as a Chinese scholar, and made such an impact upon the Chinese that another church of one hundred thousand was planted. While this contextualization of the gospel is established missionary practice today, it ran counter to the "God's will!" certainty of the age in Europe, and when a Dominican and Franciscan came to China to inspect the work, they recoiled in horror at what they found. The church in China collapsed under their attempt to reform it.

Meanwhile the church Xavier had left behind in Japan was stamped out by the same shogun who closed Japan to European influence for hundreds of years. While Jesuit practices in Europe during this time were questionable, the Jesuits and other Catholic orders were way ahead of Protestants in missions.

THE SPIRITUAL EXERCISES

Loyola was a strict disciplinarian. When one of his founding members sought to lead the Jesuits in Portugal in a manner different from his assignment, Loyola fired the man and had him banished. Loyola saw one way of doing things, and he was passionately committed to having his instructions followed.

These instructions were laid down in his *Spiritual Exercises.* This book, the foundation of the Jesuit experience, is like a boot camp for the soul. The exercises are powerful—a disciplined method for growing closer to God. In fact, it is difficult to find a more pointed, beautiful, spiritually rich guide to spiritual growth than this classic, written by a Spanish knight who had given himself wholly to Jesus. In this day of Christian bookstores and large Christian publishing houses, *The Spiritual Exercises* remains an exceptionally pointed teaching plan for leading new Christians to Christ or older Christians to a deeper walk with Christ.

Born out of Loyola's own passionate experience, the exercises are designed to build a passion for Jesus through imaginative meditation. But rather than the imitation of the simple love of Jesus that we see in Francis, Loyola's book is a tough-minded guide for the spiritual and psychological preparation of a knight of Christ. The exercises are evocative. At times they seem harsh. At one point they call upon the student to imagine the horrible howls of people screaming in hell. But Loyola wanted those doing these exercises to be *moved*, and if the student wasn't moved, then Loyola believed he wasn't doing them right.

It is a teacher's book in that it was written to guide the director of a Christian's spiritual journey rather than the student alone. There are instructions to the director to adapt the exercises to the context of the learner (and indeed Ignatian spiritual directors today have a much less military approach that fits our times better). Still, the goal of the exercises is to create mentally strong disciples who will practice "taking every thought captive" (2 Corinthians 10:5, NASB) in pursuit of a life wholly given over to Jesus.

LIKE CALVIN

Although Loyola and Calvin were on opposite sides of the great holy war of the Reformation, they shared much the same attitude toward the demands of the faith. Set aside at an early age for the service of God, they each pursued other skills that shaped the men they became—Calvin the law and Loyola the art of war. Students in the same crucible of learning at the University of Paris, they did not accept what they were taught as the last word but pressed on with determination and originality to reform the church as they saw it. Both were practical leaders in a time of spiritual conflict. Both wrote tough-minded, logical works intended to mold the minds of practical ministers. Both could be tough disciplinarians when faced with what they perceived as disorder among those they led.

They were passionate men who nevertheless took their passions captive through their strict application of the logical mind and were hated by many for doing so. They were both absolutely certain that they knew—and could teach others to know—God's will. History has demonstrated that they were both at least partly right. And both continue to influence Christians today. What can we apply to our themes from their experience?

People Like Us

Both Calvin and Loyola were definitely human. They were hard men in a hard time who played hardball with their opponents. But they were also men of great faith and fortitude who overcame chronic health problems to build vigorous organizations for expanding the kingdom of God. Too bad the organizations they formed became locked in mortal combat for the next three hundred years.

The Body of Christ and the Human Institution

Both Calvin and Loyola saw clearly the need for reformation in order to become more the body of Christ. They each wrote about this need. They each sought to apply this reform to the bodies they formed and led. But they moved in diametrically opposite directions in their understanding of the authority of Rome. And—like the Franciscans and Lutherans before them—their organizations institutionalized their flaws as well as their strengths. Do we see a pattern here? Is it a pattern we can do anything about?

Faith Versus Reason

Both Calvin and Loyola had great faith in God, but both saw the necessity of harnessing reason to explain and further that faith. During this period reason was replacing faith as the primary currency of the mind. You could argue that each was *forced* to embrace and emphasize reason in order to win a hearing. They each did so with aplomb.

If we are to learn from them, we would do well not to apply their sixteenth-century reason without examining its context. Instead, our question probably ought to be, "What constitutes effective rationalism in our time, and how do we apply the gospel to it?" As Ricci learned in China, we can be much more successful in communicating the gospel if we do so in terms that the culture around us can understand.

One of the great theological debates that emerged from Calvin's reasoned attempt to make sense of the Scriptures continues to echo in churches today. One side of the debate is summarized in the five points of TULIP (see pages 167-168), which actually emerged from the Reformed churches in Holland during the Synod of Dort in 1618. The other was articulated by Jacob Arminius, who questioned the hard-edged logic that states that God elects some for salvation and therefore predestines others for damnation.

Arminius argued that God's election is based on his foreknowledge of those who will choose salvation. Rather than believing that Christ's sacrifice on the cross applied only to the elect (limited atonement), he said Christ died for all but only believers obtain any benefit. That difference depends on the sinner's action not on God's action. Salvation, then, is based on a free choice of the individual's will, not on the irresistible grace of an absolutely sovereign God.

The logic of this view requires the next step: The will of the individual believer controls God's grace. If the believer later decides to reject God's salvation and stops believing (or stops *behaving* like a Christian), then salvation can be lost. It can be restored only by the individual's conscious choice to return to God through repentance. This view edges into salvation by works—the work being the act of belief by the returning sinner. While the Synod of Dort rejected these ideas, many continued to hold them, and later John Wesley found in them a better explanation of his own spiritual experience than he did in Calvinism.

Both Calvin's and Arminius's reasoning rest on impeccable logic applied to *selected* Scriptures—and yet they are diametrically opposed. How can this happen? Is Scripture inconsistent with itself? Do we need to ignore the parts of it that don't agree with our view? Or do we need to suspend our rationalism in the face of God's mystery, which we won't understand completely this side of death? You decide. But I pray that whatever view your mind and heart leads you to accept, you won't start to regard those who disagree with you as spiritual enemies. Satan loves that.

Church + State = Very Bad Things

By this time the danger of a tight wrapping of the church together with the state ought to be plain to us. It wasn't, however, to either Calvin or Loyola, because the tradition from which they both came had stopped questioning the assumption that this was God's will. Others in Europe at this time—the so-called "radical reformers"—were questioning this assumption, and the results of their questions were many new groups persecuted by both Catholics and Protestants. Ultimately these groups, forced out of Europe by these persecutions, had an enormous influence in the New World.

What About Missions?

Depending on your viewpoint, this was a wonderful or a terrible time for missions. In my own denomination, we invest much energy in training and sending young people out during school break as "summer missionaries." There's an old joke that says of summer missionaries: "Well you know, summer missionaries, and summer not." Perhaps we ought to say the same of the Catholic missionaries of this period. While some were not much more than baptized conquistadors, others sacrificed their lives for the sake of the gospel. While some of the churches they founded were flawed, many of those churches grew to form great Christian leaders on their own.

Calvin's record on missions was better than Luther's. True, most of his efforts focused on training leaders who returned to their native lands and established Reformed cells there. One such was John Knox of Scotland, whose work led to the Presbyterian Church.

Unlike Luther, Calvin did authorize the sending of some missionaries to the newly discovered lands of South America. Not that they were very successful: There they met some Catholic missionaries who arrested them and had them killed. How sad it is when God's people spend their energies attacking one another, rather than seeking to love those who don't know Christ.

Ethics Optional?

Both Calvin and Loyola reacted with vehemence against the immorality of the church of their time. Both demanded moral living from themselves and their followers. That was their ideal. Of course, Calvinists and Jesuits each accused the other of the worst ethical offences. In fact, in reading about these two groups, it's valuable to first check the bias of your sources, because the bias against both Calvin and Loyola runs *extremely* high. Still, there is evidence that the spiritual descendents of both men practiced—at least to some degree—that old ethical caveat, "The end justifies the means."

Nowhere was this attitude more blatantly in evidence than in the next place we must look. Hold on. We're jumping into the deep end of the pool: the English Reformation.

WANT TO KNOW MORE?

The best place to begin to understand each of these great figures is in their own writings. Read Calvin's *Institutes of the Christian Religion*. It remains a classic of Protestant theology, and among Reformed churches is perhaps *the* classic. There are also many biographies of Calvin, a good one being Bernard Cottret's *Calvin: A Biography* (Grand Rapids, MI: Eerdmans, 1995; English translation, 2000). Then there's no better place to begin to understand Loyola than by reading through—and perhaps even prayerfully doing—his *Spiritual Exercises*. There's an excellent little book by a Jesuit that explains the exercises in context called *Virtuous Passions: The Formation of Christian Character* by G. Simon Harak (Mahwah, NJ: Paulist Press, 1993).

All English, All Certain

CRANMER, CROMWELL, AND BUNYAN

Henry VIII had a problem. (Actually, Henry VIII *was* a problem. Charles Dickens called him a "most intolerable ruffian and a blot of blood and grease on the history of England," which pretty well sums it up.) To paraphrase a cliché, if Henry wasn't happy, nobody was happy. Or safe. This was a time when "keeping your head on straight" had an entirely different meaning than it does today. Henry tended to behead those who (formerly) worked for him or who (formerly) were married to him.

Henry's problem was that his wife, Catherine of Aragon, hadn't given him a male heir. Without such an heir, the country risked descending into the bloody battles over the throne that had racked England before Henry's father took control. Catherine had been briefly married to Henry's brother, who had died young, and Henry thought Catherine's lack of sons was a divine curse for violating Leviticus 20:21. He wanted his pet cardinal (Cardinal Wolsey) to get the pope to give him a divorce.

The pope, however, couldn't do it. He was under the control of the Holy Roman Emperor, Charles V, and Catherine was Charles's aunt. The pope and the emperor were dealing with other problems: Muslim Turks attacking in the east and the impudent Luther in the north. The pope didn't say no immediately, because he didn't want to lose English money, but he couldn't say yes.

Catherine couldn't deliver the heir Henry wanted; Cardinal Wolsey couldn't deliver the divorce Henry wanted. They both had to go. Despite Wolsey's long toadying service, Henry had him stripped of his power, which had been considerable. Wolsey died soon thereafter — some say from pure frustration.

Then Henry heard the idea of a priest named Thomas Cranmer. Cranmer suddenly found himself in Henry's service, applying his solution, which was to ask theologians of European universities to give their views of Henry's problem. While not all agreed that the pope had erred in allowing Henry to marry his brother's wife, enough of them did that Cranmer was able to tell Henry what he wanted to hear: He could divorce Catherine and marry the woman who (currently) held his attention, Anne Boleyn. To do so, Henry had to break the government of the English church away from Roman Catholic control. Historians date the birth of the English Reformation from Henry's action.

There *was* a genuine spiritual reformation in England, but it certainly didn't start with Henry's lust. Still, his lust was what gave the Reformers widespread influence. Henry was Catholic. The pope had even given him the title "Defender of the Faith" for writing an attack on Luther's heresy. He regularly attended Mass — when it didn't interfere with his hunting. He never really wanted to change the church; he just wanted to control it.

But in wresting that control away from the popes by breaking with Rome, he opened the door for the independently minded English to think for themselves, and the real English Reformation flooded through. Henry tried later to stopper it back up, but he couldn't. He didn't start the Reformation in England—John Wycliffe, William Tyndale, and others had already done that by translating the Bible into English. He certainly couldn't stop it when it suited his whim to do so. Nor, by that time, did Cranmer want him to. Cranmer had become—almost by accident—a great Reformer.

THOMAS CRANMER
1489–1556

Born the son of a poor member of the gentry, Thomas was marked for service to the church when his father could only afford to support his older brother. Educated at Cambridge, he was forced to go to Essex by a plague. There he came to the attention of Henry VIII and made the suggestion that eventually prompted Henry to break with Rome. Henry made him archbishop of Canterbury.

As he aided Henry in revising English church practice, Cranmer became more Protestant in his views and promoted them. He helped write the Forty-Two Articles that distanced the Anglican church from Rome, which later became the Thirty-Nine Articles that guide Anglicans today. He also wrote the *Book of Common Prayer*, which has bound the Anglican church together. At Henry's death, Cranmer became even more influential on the young Edward VI. He was imprisoned by Queen Mary and forced to recant his Protestant views, but as he was being executed he shouted afresh his Protestant sympathies, damaging Mary's ability to turn the English church back to Rome.

CHAMELEON?

Cranmer is an interesting study in the personal battle between conforming to society's pressures and living out one's own convictions. A less generous treatment of him might suggest that he was a chameleon, changing his spiritual color to match the religious background of the day, but I don't think that does justice to his inner struggle. He genuinely believed in God and (ultimately) Lutheran theology, but, based on his understanding of Romans 13, he believed that the king should rule the church. He also was, by turns, both courageous and cowardly. Most people are, when you get right down to it.

The young Cranmer studied at Cambridge, but when he married a local tavern-keeper's daughter upon his graduation, he lost both his scholarship and his chance at the priesthood. When she died in childbirth, however, the university accepted him back. He was a practicing Catholic, studying for the priesthood, yet he was also a part of that circle at Cambridge mockingly referred to as "Little Germany" because of its fascination with Luther. He became recognized as an excellent scholar and writer, and, despite any Protestant leanings, he became a priest in 1523.

In 1529 he was staying in Essex to avoid a plague in Cambridge when his comments about how Henry might escape his marriage came to the king's ears. Suddenly the farmer's-son-turned-scholar had become a central figure in world politics, and Henry VIII wanted results. After providing Henry with the academic opinion he desired, Cranmer was sent to Germany as an ambassador to the Holy Roman Emperor specifically to argue the case for Henry's divorce. He was also able to study further the Lutheran ideas he found so attractive. And he found an attractive young woman there—

Margaret—and married her. He hid his wife when he got home, but you have to figure this was yet another driving force in his own embrace of (noncelibate) Protestantism.

Anne Boleyn was pregnant by this time, and Henry was desperate to marry her. He appointed Cranmer the archbishop of Canterbury, and Cranmer declared him to be legally divorced. Thomas married Henry to Anne, and they all lived happily ever after—or would have, had Anne given Henry a son instead of the baby who would become Elizabeth I. (It's ironic that Henry went through all this because he didn't think a queen would be strong enough to govern England, yet Queen Elizabeth went on to become one of the most powerful English monarchs.)

When Anne failed a second time to produce a son, Henry decided he needed to move on. Anne was accused of adultery and beheaded. The king told Cranmer that Elizabeth had been conceived outside of marriage, and Cranmer again did what the king wanted and declared that marriage null. Henry married Anne of Cleves. Whom he found repugnant. So Cranmer declared that marriage null because it had taken place unlawfully because Henry had actually really been married to Anne Boleyn.

All right, so at this point Cranmer does sound like nothing but Henry's gofer. But he also stood up to the king and pleaded for the lives of Thomas More and John Fisher, who had denied that the king had the right to disobey the pope. They still died—but he tried. So what did Cranmer really do with the influence he maintained by saying yes to Henry?

REMAKING THE CHURCH

For one thing, he remade the English church in a Protestant image. Using the currency gained by agreeing to Henry's less-than-Christian understanding of marriage (Henry would likely have done what he wanted regardless), Cranmer set about changing the church into what he truly believed it should be. When Henry felt that the reforms were moving too far from his own Catholic preference, the king forced new reforms through Parliament to turn back the clock. Cranmer opposed him. Remarkably, he survived. And when Henry was about to die, he wanted Thomas Cranmer beside him.

EDWARD VI

When Henry's son Edward came to the throne, things changed again. Now Cranmer had the freedom to do what he believed should be done, and he went to work. He wrote the Forty-Two Articles (including the freedom for clergy to marry), which Parliament adopted, officially bringing the English church into the Protestant camp.

Concerned that the people needed more effective biblical preaching, Cranmer also wrote the *Book of Homilies*. He wrote the *Book of Common Prayer*—twice, actually, once with a more Protestant slant and once with a more Catholic slant—to provide worship forms for the English church in the English language. In this he had an enormous influence on the development of the English language itself, as well as on English theology, because he was a master stylist and because everybody in England was required to attend church weekly and hear his words.

These were his greatest contributions. Then Edward died.

Almighty and most merciful Father, we have erred and strayed
from thy ways like lost sheep. We have followed too much the
devices and desires of our own hearts.

THOMAS CRANMER, *BOOK OF COMMON PRAYER*

IMPRISONED BY MARY

Mary, Henry's daughter by Catherine, became queen. Queen
Mary revoked the Articles. (She was Catherine's daughter and
a fierce Catholic—who can blame her after the way Henry
treated her and her mother?) But despite Mary's opposition,
Cranmer reworked his principles into the Thirty-Nine Articles,
the foundation of the Anglican faith today. Mary had no use
for Cranmer. He had been the one, after all, who had declared
her mother divorced from Henry and who had married her
father to Anne Boleyn. He'd also backed the claim of Lady
Jane Grey to the throne in defiance of Mary's legitimate claim.
She had him arrested for treason and held him in prison for
eighteen months.

This is the Mary that George Foxe dubbed "Bloody Mary"
in his book of martyrs. She was probably kinder than history
has remembered her, but she was certainly determined to return
England to the Catholic fold, and more than three hundred
Protestants died in her attempt. After his long imprisonment,
Cranmer signed statements recanting his Protestant views—in
hopes of saving his life. When at last Mary determined he
should die for his heresies, Cranmer was given the opportunity
to publically renounce his Protestant views, but when he took
to the pulpit he spoke from his heart instead of from his fear.

He publically recanted his signed recantation of his Protestant faith. Before he was cut off by his surprised captors, he spoke his best-remembered line. Waving his hand, he said, "This is the hand that signed it, so it shall suffer first punishment." He was dragged away to the stake and set on fire, and he suffered his death courageously according to eyewitnesses. But as he promised, he symbolically thrust his hand into the blaze first. What Mary had hoped to accomplish by his death was foiled, and Thomas Cranmer was canonized as a saint of the Anglican Church.

Was he a wishy-washy coward or a man constantly at war between his lesser self and his own integrity? Probably both. There are few people who are *not* both, at least in some measure. But throughout a life lived constantly under the pressure of kings, queens, and conscience, he did his best to accomplish what good he could within the allowances of time and culture. And he did a great deal; he, more than anyone else, shaped the Anglican Church.

TURBULANCE

Any surfer can tell you that when you're riding the crest of a wave, there's an exhilirating sense of power. When you're crushed *under* the wave, however, in the turbulent whirling and spinning of that salty, sandy water, it's not much fun. The English Reformation was turbulent: During the period between Henry's break from Rome and the crowning of Elizabeth I, the English people were expected to be Protestant for three years, then (doctrinally) Catholic for seven years when Henry decided to return to Catholic practice, then Protestant again for six and a half years under his son Edward VI, then Catholic again for five years under Mary, then back to Protestant under the new Queen Elizabeth. It would be enough to give anyone spiritual whiplash.

This was all the result of the emerging European understanding that the religion of the people ought to match that of their ruler. Why? Shall we fault Constantine? So closely had religion become tied to the government that this must have seemed the natural answer. This was already the solution being worked out in Luther's Germany—the people of a province followed the religious wishes of their prince. Not yet were governments thinking that people ought to be allowed to practice the religion of their *preference*, of their *conscience*. The concept of religious freedom was to be one of the greatest contributions of the English Reformation, but it took years to get to that point.

There were, however, many English believers who were already privately expressing their own convictions. This was hastened by the distribution of English-language Bibles, a process Henry at first encouraged then sought to cut off when he realized people were thinking for themselves. But the process had begun. The result was the formation of multiple denominations of believers, including, besides Anglicans, the British Presbyterians (organizationally separate from Scottish Presbyterians), Congregationalists, Baptists, and Quakers. These groups came to be known collectively in England as Separatists because they separated themselves from the Anglican Church.

Many believers in these groups held to a severe lifestyle that resulted in their being called Puritans—forerunners of groups that powerfully influenced American history. Many leaders in these new churches fled to the Netherlands to escape persecution and death, and it was there that one of the largest groups in America today was born.

Baptists debate when exactly the Baptist faith came into being. Some argue that there have always been true believers in the faith of the New Testament who never became organizationally linked to the Roman Catholic Church. A pamphlet called "The Trail of Blood" sketched out how these groups — identified primarily by their rejection of infant baptism — maintained their separation down through the centuries, often in hiding, at other times enduring persecution. The historical accuracy of this viewpoint is challenged by the fact that some of the groups cited as "baptistic" by the pamphlet were, in fact, far from orthodox.

Still, there is no question that there were often dissenters. During the Swiss Reformation (see chapter 8), some of the strong supporters of Ulrich Zwingli (one of the primary Swiss Reformers) raised objection to baptizing babies. They were convicted of heresy and drowned. Those who opposed infant baptism came to be known as Anabaptists (rebaptizers), because they refused to accept as members anyone who did not make a conscious and public profession of faith in Christ that included adult baptism. These groups, which sprang up all across Europe independently, are ususally referred to as the Radical Reformation.

Most historians trace the beginnings of present-day Baptists to the Separatist John Smythe, who had himself rebaptized while in exile in Holland in the early 1600s. The church that formed around him moved back to England about the same time as another Separatist group in Holland — the people Americans know as the Pilgrims — departed for the New World in the *Mayflower*. While Smythe later left the Baptist church he helped to form, other Baptist churches began to spring up. Since Baptists have generally resisted any kind of top-down governance (this attitutde is called the "free church tradition"), it's difficult to trace their growth with precision. From the point of view of the Anglican leadership, they were yet another part of those Separatists that proved so difficult to control.

The Separatists differed from one another on key issues but were generally united on the critical importance of the Scriptures. This diversity of thought continued for two hundred years, with first one group and then another leading the opposition to the Anglican-Catholic viewpoint. Queen Elizabeth minimized the conflict by holding a moderating course between them, apparently because she held no strong religious views herself. But when she passed from the scene without an heir, James VI of Scotland became James I of England and united the two countries. The battles began anew. Real battles.

TO CIVIL WAR

Americans think of the Civil War as the War Between the States, the North-versus-South conflict that resolved the issues of states' rights and slavery. To the English, however, the term applies to the religious war of the 1600s. The stage was set for this war by the people's expectations of King James—and by his own attitudes.

Everyone in England had high hopes when James took the English throne: Catholics knew he was married to a Catholic and held strong personal religious views. Anglicans expected him to carry on the Protestant tradition of Elizabeth. Separatists expected that because he came from Scotland, where Calvinist Presbyterians had long before been firmly established by John

Knox, he would be responsive to their views. In fact, this last group met with him as he made his way to London to take the throne, and won from him the concession of a new English Bible translation. We know it as the King James Version. It was largely a complilation of the existing English Bible versions and has passed through numerous revisions down through the years.

This, however, was the most the Separatists got out of James, and the other groups didn't get much more. The reason? James *was* very religious—and absolutely certain that he had been made king by God's divine appointment. He believed in the divine right of kings to make the rules, and he set about doing so, frustrating all the groups as he did. He infuriated Separatists by insisting that sports and entertainments could take place on Sundays. He failed to move the Anglican Church any closer to the pope, preferring to control things as they were. He let it be known that his relationships with the Scottish Presbyterians had never been cordial because they insisted on their own way. He was fairly tolerant of Catholics until 1605, when Guy Fawkes and others—including some Jesuits—were implicated in a plot to blow up Parliament, usually called the Gunpowder Plot. James sharply restricted Roman Catholic activities from this point. All of this he did with an arrogant, autocratic air that infuriated the English Parliament, who'd had some taste of freedom and didn't like being dictated to one bit. But it was when James died and his son Charles came to the throne that the great break occurred. This time it cost the *king* his head.

Charles I wasn't a good manager; he was constantly running out of money. He wasn't a very astute politician, either; he always seemed to back the losing side. He was a strong believer, but he was a Catholic, and he married a Catholic princess over Parliament's objections. He tried to control Parliament until Parliament decided to control him, and open war broke out between the supporters of the crown and the supporters of Parliament. The leader of Parliament's army had been a member of Parliament. He was one of those figures that pop up infrequently through history as part of a small but powerful fraternity—military geniuses that rise to absolute power. Beside Alexander, Julius Caesar, Constantine, and Charlemagne stands Oliver Cromwell.

OLIVER CROMWELL
1599–1658

A farmer for his first forty years, Cromwell had a conversion experience in his late twenties that radicalized his life. A Puritan, he became a member of a mostly Presbyterian Parliament that opposed King Charles I. Joining Parliament's army, he rose to become general and redesigned its tactics and strategies. Most of his soldiers were Separatists like himself, and he made of each battle a holy war. He won them all — some in very bloody fashion. When Charles lost the war but refused to toe the line, Cromwell had him beheaded and became the Lord Protector of England. He held dictatorial power until his death and remains a controversial figure, admired by some and hated by others — much as he was throughout his life.

OLIVER CROMWELL

Oliver Cromwell was born into a farm family near Cambridge and thrust into adult responsibilities at sixteen when his father died. He spoke little, but when he did, his words were weighted with importance. At around twenty-seven he had a deep conversion experience and became a zealous Puritan. When he was made justice of the peace, he demonstrated a determination and quiet power that settled issues quickly—in his favor.

His quiet personal power came to the attention of the local Puritan elders, and they elected him to Parliament. His first term was short—only three weeks—for when King Charles realized that the (mostly Presbyterian) body was not going to rubber stamp his requests, he dismissed it, determined to rule without parliamentary authority. This was called the Short Parliament. But when Charles realized he needed Parliament if he wanted any chance of getting money, he called another Parliament that sat for many years—the Long Parliament—and Cromwell returned to government.

The Long Parliament was even less inclined to agree with the king than the Short Parliament had been, and when it refused to disband, Charles tried to force the issue with an army. The result was war, and Cromwell joined Parliament's army—what came to be called the New Model Army—against the king's forces. Cromwell had no prior military training, but he did know how to handle horses from his years on the farm, and he helped to organize a cavalry division that proved extremely effective. The key was discipline, which Cromwell had the character to enforce.

As the hostilities broadened, he rose through the ranks to become captain, and recruited and trained a thousand soldiers who came to be known by Cromwell's own nickname, the Ironsides. He recruited Separatists like himself and made the battle with the king a holy war. His forces prayed before each encounter and rode into battle singing hymns. His main tactic was to break through the enemy's center line with his cavalry, then flank them either to the right or left and encircle them. It proved sucessful again and again.

Eventually Cromwell became general. When King Charles invited the Catholic Irish to join him as allies, Cromwell conquered them, allowing massacres of the enemy in the name of God. King Charles was defeated and captured, but he wouldn't cooperate with Parliament. Instead, he escaped London and this time enlisted the Presbyterian Scots to fight for him. Cromwell smashed the Scots as well, and the king was recaptured.

Cromwell had come to believe that the king's death was God's will. This time Charles was put on trial and executed, leaving the English government without a leader. Experience had prepared Cromwell to lead—so he did.

He refused the crown that was offered to him but accepted instead the title of Lord Protector and governed as a dictator. He tolerated religious differences—to a point—but could be intolerant of individuals who crossed him, whatever their religious affiliation. He expanded trade, waged some successful external wars, and strengthened the power of the British Isles versus the rest of Europe. But while he was certainly feared, he wasn't loved. The Commonwealth he put in place disintegrated after his death, when his weak-willed son became Lord Protector. After years of war and Puritan rule, the people were clamoring again for a king, and the Restoration placed James II on the throne. Cromwell's bones were dug up from Westminster Abbey, hanged, and burned. Not that Cromwell was there to be bothered by it.

Why include Cromwell among those greats of history who changed the church? After all, while he won many battles and ruled England, none of his changes lasted. He wasn't a theologian—not even a churchman. What did he do, after all?

One of the dates I was forced to memorize as a child was the establishment of the Plymouth colony in 1620. The Pilgrims who sailed to America did so in response to the same religious intolerance that prompted Cromwell's personal rebellion. After their successful landing, a flood of Puritan refugees sailed to New England—people of the same thought and spirit as Cromwell. They must have rejoiced when they heard about the success of the Puritan general in the Civil War and the new English Commonwealth where they would not be persecuted for their beliefs. Perhaps many felt the lure to return to the newly freed (from their perspective, anyway) England. But Cromwell's experiment didn't last. It did, however, provide a model for the future. It would be more than a hundred years before the children's children of those religious refugees would take arms against their king as Cromwell had and win, but the pattern had been set. Warriors of God could triumph over the tyranny of the wealthy aristocracy.

Another part of Cromwell's legacy was the importance of the committed layperson. It would be the laity that made the real difference in the growth of Congregational, Baptist, and (eventually) Methodist churches of the next generation. Sturdy character and pietistic zeal would become of chief importance. We'll hear more about those in our next chapter, but first there's one more individual who deserves some special attention. For while Cromwell wrote his legacy with a sword, John Bunyan wrote his with a pen in prison, and his *Pilgrim's Progress* altered the way his English-language readers regarded the Christian journey.

JOHN BUNYAN
1628–1688

An English Baptist preacher and writer, he was a part of Cromwell's army from 1644 to 1647. After becoming a Separatist through an experience of personal conversion in 1653, he was baptized into the Baptist church in Bedford, his hometown. He became a deacon in 1655 and began preaching, and was arrested for preaching without a license in 1658. He persisted in preaching until he was jailed in 1660, and for most of the next twelve years he remained in jail, preaching through the bars and writing. Although he wrote several books, by far his best received and most widely distributed was *Pilgrim's Progress*, which remains a Christian classic.

BUNYAN, BRIEFLY

Is the pen mightier than the sword? Certainly Luther's writings set fire to Europe, Calvin's writings have endured to the present, and Cranmer's *Book of Common Prayer* caused more lasting change in the religious beliefs of England than did the furious dictates of Henry VIII. Actually, who cares which is more powerful? Both the pen and the sword have had their place in Christian history, and Bunyan wielded both in his lifetime. He fought in Cromwell's army, so his early inclinations must have been toward the Separatist viewpoint, but it wasn't until 1653 that he actually became a member of a Baptist church.

It's doubtful from his writings, however, if Bunyan was as much a Baptist as he was a Christian. He had little patience for the debates of denominations. His passion was the internal relationship of the individual heart with God. That he could be stubborn in defense of his right to share this basic message is clear from his record of imprisonment.

After the Restoration of the monarchy, the new king and his agreeable Parliament set out to return things to the way they'd been before Cromwell, but Bunyan would have none of it. In a time when the key idea in returning to religious uniformity was to force all preachers to obtain appropriate licensure through the established Church of England, Bunyan continually asserted what he thought was his calling, to tell people what he believed. He just wouldn't quit. He still didn't quit when they locked him up. For more than a decade, he remained in prison, when he could have walked out free just by agreeing not to preach anymore. Instead, he preached through the bars of his cell, and people came to hear him. He must have been a thoroughly frustrating prisoner to his jailors.

But his greatest sermon was one he wrote: a lengthy allegorical story called *Pilgrim's Progress*. It's about a character named Christian who grew miserable living in the City of Destruction and struck out toward the Celestial City, unsure of what he might meet along the way. Avoiding the Slough of Despond (depression), he made it through the Wicket Gate and onto the straight and narrow road. When he came to the foot of the cross, the burden of sins he had been carrying in a knapsack on his back fell away. From that point forward the journey was one of growth in spiritual discipline and warfare in places like Vanity Fair (materialism), until he came at last to his heavenly destination.

This book struck a chord with Bunyan's audience and became one of the most widely read works ever printed in English. It is sometimes thought of as the first English novel, and its references became so pervasive in popular culture that it remains an important work today.

THE ENGLISH LEGACY

By the late 1600s the English Reformation had forever altered the Christian landscape. What began in Henry's fit of pique had dispersed Bibles and other Christian writings in English and boosted the English educational level. Multiple Christian perspectives became widespread and held strongly enough to form separate denominations, all adamantly fixed on the truth of their own interpretation of Scripture. Battles and persecutions had scattered Christians of various stripes to North America and beyond.

The monarchy had been destroyed by Christian rebels and restored by Christian conservatives, but when James II tried to move the land back toward Roman Catholicism, all parties in Parliament united to drive him from the country and invite his Protestant daughter Mary and her husband, William, to invade England and claim the throne. This was called the Glorious Revolution, and it fixed the English government as Protestant from that day forward.

As for the spiritual condition of the nation—well, that was going to come under far more pressure from rationalism and the Enlightenment than it had from warring denominations. It's time to talk of the rise of the intellect—and the corresponding response of pietism. But first: how did the tumultuous English Reformation affect our six themes?

People Like Us

Cranmer, Cromwell, Bunyan—were these people like us? They were certainly different from one another in their personalities, their place in history, and their religious understandings. But they were people like us in that they struggled to understand the same questions, to exercise their free wills in following their consciences, and to make a difference in the face of a society that held differing views and sought to force those views upon them.

This book has focused primarily on important individuals who affected the churches of their time, and these were certainly that. At the same time, this period moves us ever closer to our present consciousness of both the importance of the individual and his or her relative insignificance against the tide of history. There are fewer giants but many more giant killers, if you will. While these three may be representative of the thoughts of many others in their time, they represent also the growing voice of the people in the church. Whether they were indeed people like us, we are certainly potentially people like them.

The Body of Christ and the Human Institution

The struggle between the church as the body of Christ or as a human institution became a core idea of this period. There were multiple interpretations of what it meant to be Christ's body and what should be the nature of the church as an institution. A result was that *many* churches emerged from this period with strongly defined beliefs of what being the body of Christ meant, and these churches largely rejected all views but their own. These rejections of other Christians became institutionalized into the fabric of the denominations in ways that have only begun to fade during the last fifty years. The body of Christ became "us," and the human institution was "everybody else."

Faith Versus Reason

During this period, the assumptions of the Renaissance moved toward the triumph of the intellect in the Enlightenment. Reason replaced faith as the foundation for understanding truth. Faith came to be regarded as narrow, rigid dogma, reinforced by the burning of those who disagreed. Little wonder that those who exercised their minds toward free thought felt repulsed by faith. At the same time, there was much faith expressed—with great certainty—by all parties in the English Reformation, even when that faith threatened the unity of the institutional church.

To enlarge this discussion we would have to spend much time defining faith and reason as various leaders, speakers, and writers understood them. Perhaps it's better just to recognize that during this time of religious-intellectual ferment, many people meant very different things by those words. The time of sharpened intellectual—and spiritual—definitions was still to come.

Church + State = Very Bad Things

Battles, burnings, and beheadings proliferated—on all sides. Every faction had its shot at ruling, and every faction demonstrated as much willingness to kill for Christ as they had to die for him. The English Reformation produced many bad things, mostly because Catholics, Protestants, and Separatists all wanted to control the church through the state. This was partly why the emerging American experiment placed so much value on the separation of the church from the state. Freedom to worship as one chose was destined to became a primary right when that new republic emerged.

What About Missions?

While the religious struggle in England and elsewhere in Europe continued, so too did the colonization of—quite literally—the world. Along with merchants and sailors there went religious leaders, some of whom recognized the need to tell conquered peoples the gospel of Christ. But it must have been difficult to share the joy of that gospel with people who were being pushed down and shoved out by the messengers themselves. Colonization tainted missions to varying degrees for a long time.

Ethics Optional?

Were the leaders of the English Reformation ethical? All of them sought to be, in their own way (well, we might need to make an exception for Henry VIII). At the same time, we might argue with many of the actions of the leaders we've focused on. Did Cranmer show character in approving serial divorce in order to accomplish positive reforms? Or was he a coward? Cromwell was certainly no coward, but did he exercise vengeful brutality in his actions against the Irish and King Charles? He probably didn't think so. Would Bunyan have been more a blessing to his family if he had agreed to limit his preaching—perhaps to just what he wrote—and lived and worked at home?

While we might second-guess these figures, we do so in the clarity of hindsight. They were dealing with the realities of their own lives in real time, on a day-to-day basis. If we're going to criticize them, we'd best be wary of what succeeding generations might say of us. Then again—isn't that what this book is about? To rethink Christian history for the light it can shed on our own concerns and decisions?

WANT TO KNOW MORE?

Why not read *Pilgrim's Progress*? It's one of the great works of Christian literature—really, of world literature—and while it came from the pen of Bunyan the Baptist, it was a product of the whole of the English Reformation. You might also read some of the *Book of Common Prayer* and find there the seed—or even the full expression—of words and ideas you've heard in church all your life but never knew the source. For the rest, the English Reformation was an extremely complicated phenomenon, intricately tied into two hundred years of English history. A good church history text or even just a good world history might give you an overview that would help you determine areas of specific interest. You'll find a great variety of personalities and viewpoints to choose from.

10

Moravians, Methodists, and Missions

VON ZINZENDORF, CAREY, AND WESLEY

Think of the great rivers of the world: the Mississippi, the Nile, the Amazon. Each of these flows for many miles as a mighty, unified waterway—until it nears the ocean. Then it divides as if different parts of the river suddenly developed radically different viewpoints and can no longer bear to remain in the same bed. The river divides into a vast delta as each of these different-minded rivulets struggles to find its own way to the sea.

History is like that—church history especially. While we can (sort of) see a single river of relationship rolling forward into the future from the first century, with the coming of the Reformation, the history of the church breaks apart. The story can appear to be more about the disagreements between the streams than about the life-giving water carried by all. Perhaps it just appears that way to us since we can't see into the future.

Perhaps we are so close to more recent history that we don't have the perspective to see the unity in Christian diversity.

In the chapters remaining, we will focus on church history as it most affects the primary audience of this book, younger evangelical Christians in Europe and North America. Much has happened in Catholic and Orthodox churches over the past five centuries, but we're going to focus on Protestants. And although today the church is booming far more in the Southern Hemisphere than in Europe or North America, we're not going to give Christianity in the Global South anything like the coverage it deserves.

There are several major clusters of ideas that have had a maximum impact on the evangelical church of the present. They are pietism, revivalism, ecumenism, Pentecostalism, and chiliasm. Maybe you know or can guess what those first four are but have no idea what the last means.

Chiliasm does not mean strong support for a long, narrow country on the west coast of South America, nor does it mean advocating one side of the great meat-or-no-meat debate concerning a hot Tex-Mex bean stew. Chiliasm is the technical term for great concern regarding the details of Christ's thousand-year reign on earth. It's sometimes called millennialism. While chiliasm has been in the church since the Montanists back in the 200s, it became a focus of much church energy about 160 years ago and has continued to grow in importance.

These sets of ideas became major players because of advocates, individuals who have represented the idea as having vast importance to the Lord and his church. Pietism came first, and together with revivalism it birthed the missions movement that planted churches around the world. But pietism came in reaction to another major cluster of ideas, widely regarded as antagonistic to the kingdom of God (and in some instances self-consciously so). This cluster is called the Enlightenment.

THE ENLIGHTENMENT

Some say we're now living in the postmodern world (although if you interviewed a dozen people on the street, few would know what that means). The Enlightenment was the beginning of the modern world, as opposed to the premodern world. From the time of Plato to the time of Luther and Calvin, Western Civilization had seen the world as fully explainable. From Paul onward, Christians framed this explanation with a mix of Hebrew and Greek ideas. The New Testament was interpreted through philosophical spectacles largely provided by Plato and Aristotle.

This tradition was all-important as the source of authority for understanding both Scripture and the world, and tradition taught a metaphysical (*beyond* the physical) dualism between the earth below and the heavens above. There was no question where humanity stood in this cosmos. On one hand, earth and its humans were the lowest, tiniest, and least significant of the celestial spheres — huge ranks of angels and powers glistened above and beyond us. On the other hand, God had given humans the highest rank in his earthly creation and had dignified us first by creating us in his image and then by sending his Son as a mortal man.

(Note that medieval people did not at all think man was the center of the universe, except in the sense that earth was the tiny and sin-stained pivot point around which the grand and pure universe revolved. "Man is the measure of all things" was the Renaissance belief that fueled both the Reformation and the Enlightenment.)

The modern world began when people began thinking outside the medieval view, questioning past revelations in the light of human reason. Just as it took many years for the Reformation to expand to its fullest influence, it took many years and many individual thinkers for the Enlightenment to become the accepted viewpoint among scholars of all areas. Because many of the activities of churches since have been (and still are) waged against the presuppositions of the Enlightenment, we really need to know something about this movement before we can see how people of faith responded to it.

THE ENLIGHTENMENT SEARCH FOR TRUTH

The basic problem the thinkers of the Enlightenment were seeking to solve is simple: If we can't trust divine revelation to tell us what is true (and the Enlightenment assumes, and sometimes tries to prove, that we can't), then how can we know what is true? Their responses began by taking sides in a longstanding philosophical debate—the distinction between myself (the subjective view) and nature (the objective view). My thinking, they recognized, rests upon both my experience of the outward world and the logical capacity of my rational mind to make sense of it. Which is most important? If we can't take the word of some inspired teaching of the past, how can we know what is really true?

Most discussions of the Enlightenment's emergence begin with the Christian humanism of Erasmus, move through Copernicus's discovery that our planet rotates around the sun, examine the thought of the Reformers, and come eventually to *René Descartes* (day-KART) (1596–1650). Descartes, a great mathematician, wanted to get down to the irreducible basics in his own thinking, so he tried to doubt everything in order to come to the truth. Rather than trusting the revelation of the past, he trusted his own experience—setting in motion what's known as empiricism. In his pursuit of truth he came to the famous bottom line, "I think, therefore I am."

While many have suggested that he should have turned that around to "I am, therefore I think," his bottom line gave him a foundation to think outward and acknowledge other things he thought to be self-evident to his reason. God was the first of those things. But while this Cartesian view supported God's existence, his new methodology opened up other very different logical interpretations as well.

Baruch Spinoza (Spe-NOUT-za) (1632–1677) appreciated Descartes' method, but came to a very different conclusion about God. Rather than the mostly orthodox God of Descartes, Spinoza decided that "God" was equivalent with the universe. The creative principle in nature was God—which to most of his critics actually meant there's no God at all. (A Jew, Spinoza was excommunicated from his synagogue.) Spinoza's self-evident conclusion was *pantheism* not theism (as Descartes had concluded). God is everything, instead of transcendent to and Creator of everything. With Descartes' empirical methodology having torn authority loose from revelation, anyone's reasoned opinion became as good as the next person's. We're still pretty much in this place today.

Another mathematician, *Blaise Pascal* (Pas-KAL) (1623–1662), took issue with the empirical methodology and advocated a return to simple faith. His point was simple: Something clear to one group may be unclear or doubtful to others—as Spinoza's views proved. Despite being extraordinarily gifted intellectually, Pascal rejected the traditional rational arguments for God's existence and emphasized the personal, relational aspects involved in coming to faith in Christ. He said, "The heart has its reasons of which reason knows not." He didn't abandon reason with reference to God—he argued that faith is *not* irrational—but he also didn't want to overvalue it. He argued that God has not revealed himself in a way that would compel faith in those who don't care or don't want to believe, so it's no surprise when some do not. The difference is faith. Pascal has therefore been called a *fideist* based on the Latin word for faith. When he died, this statement was found written on a page sewed into the lining of his coat: "God of Abraham, the God of Isaac, and the God of Jacob, and not of philosophers and men of science."

But Pascal's view didn't triumph in this time of widespread excitement about the wonder of man. *John Locke* (1632–1704), who might have become a clergyman had he not lived in an age of religious oppression, argued against the idea that we are born with ideas already in our minds. He believed in the "blank slate" mind and argued that we come to our understanding by experience (empiricism) and by our developing reason (rationalism). Locke was less certain, then, about God, although he was a believer. The knowledge we develop through our senses is never certain, but rather probable. Locke didn't discard revelation, but he believed that the only foundation for Christianity was its reasonableness, and he found all aspects of it reasonable. Whether he meant it so or not, Locke had taken a step toward "natural" religion, or the idea that religion is the natural, *reasonable* outcome of mankind's experience. While he was orthodox in his Christian belief, Locke's thinking influenced many others to move away from theism and toward deism.

Deism is the idea that the God of the Bible made the world but no longer concerns himself with it. He set the universe in motion and established natural laws that guide it, and it does not require his providential attention or interference. Deism was not atheism—it was extremely dangerous during this period to be an atheist—but deism was a step toward it, for God had been removed from daily interactions with mankind and was, in a sense, an absentee landlord. Deism rejected miracles—including the miracles of inspiration (the Bible) and resurrection (Christ). Deism became the strongest challenger to Christianity for about the next two hundred years and, in fact, was the religious belief of many of the founders of the United States of America—Benjamin Franklin, Thomas Jefferson, and Thomas Paine, to name just a few. In fact, Locke's political writings on religious toleration, basic human rights, democracy, and the right of "just revolt" came to pervade the American Constitution, so he's a very influential figure.

So too was *Isaac Newton* (1642–1727), the mathematician-astronomer who discovered differential calculus and explained the law of gravity. Newton's explanation of the laws of the physical universe had an enormous effect on men of science and went much further in dismantling the medieval view of the universe. He was not orthodox in his Christian views, instead believing in a deistic God who set in motion the laws of the universe and left them alone to operate. Suddenly deism had a scientific foundation to go along with its philosophical base.

Along with Pascal, one of the great opponents of this deistic drift was *Joseph Butler* (1692–1752), an English clergyman who responded to reason with reason. He argued that the world of nature, in which deists said they found evidence of God's natural law, was filled with moral ambiguities and contradictions. Butler used the empirical approach, focusing on facts and evidences to prove that the faith of the Bible is not irrational. Basing his conclusions on *probabilities*, as had Locke, he argued that the Bible provided a much more reasonable argument for the inconsistencies within nature than did reason and observation of the natural world. He offered a type of moral argument for the existence of the God revealed in Scripture.

Then came the Scottish skeptic *David Hume* (1711–1776). Regarding the debate between rationalism and empiricism, he argued rationality away. Reason, he said, is only a product of our experience. The principle of cause and effect, upon which so many had based so much, is just how our experience has *programmed* us to think. There really is no certainty that a particular effect will result from a particular cause—we've just associated them together by habit. We can't guarantee that the future will behave like the past, because there are no necessary connections between any two events in the universe. As to the self, while Descartes saw a simple eternal soul, Hume saw the self as a bundle of different perceptions that are constantly changing. Rationality, then, is based on empiricism, and our empirical experience is so limited we really can't be certain of anything—especially God.

In a sense Hume anticipated what's now called chaos theory, popularized by the concept of the butterfly effect (that is, a butterfly flapping his wings in West Africa can generate the beginnings of a hurricane that strikes the American coast). Hume was first and foremost a skeptic—he just didn't believe that what his experience told him was necessarily true. He angered most everybody. He attacked miracles, which enraged theists, and he disregarded the deist's ideal of a rational religion of nature. He generally discarded the "religious hypothesis" altogether. But everyone from that point on had to deal with Hume, and it's interesting to note that Hume's skepticism came to be the general perception of the modern world.

But Hume's wasn't the last word. The peak of the Enlightenment came in the writings of *Immanuel Kant* (1724–1804). Kant's *Critique of Pure Reason*, *Critique of Practical Reason*, and *Critique of Judgment* came largely in response to Hume's skeptical questions. Recognizing that we are both experiencing and thinking beings, Kant wanted to merge the ideas of rationality and empiricism together as part of the same view of human reality. Essentially he agreed with the rationalists that knowledge depends on our having *something* innate within us to make sense of the raw data of experience, but he agreed with the empiricists that we have to experience the raw data of life and the world to have something for our reason to deal with. This combination of rationality and empiricism was highly praised in its time and is today's foundation for the scientific method.

So what? This may seem to be a lot of trouble to go through to arrive at a conclusion we all take for granted. We know that we are both thinking and feeling creatures and that we use these faculties together to understand our world. The point is that we take for granted what these philosophers worked diligently to demonstrate by strictly logical methods. The Enlightenment was a time when the western world was shaking off the control of kings like James I who claimed God gave them the right to rule, and the control of churches that demanded belief in religious dogma that appeared to be — and in some cases *was* — dead. Unanimity of belief and thought was gone. This was a new world, and God was associated with the old.

Kant didn't disregard faith. In fact, he made room for it outside reason, saying that we can experience nothing in this world to prove God's existence. Belief in God was for him, instead, a practical necessity. His argument was based in morality. He thought morality was the categorical imperative for all mankind, but he said it wasn't based on knowledge of the Bible or the church or even God. Instead, knowledge of God is the *result* of moral reason.

Now, this is subtle, but think: Doesn't this understanding make God revolve around mankind, rather than mankind around God? Kant ended up saying that Jesus was really no more than the best historical example of a man living a life pleasing to God. What Kant said laid the foundation for modern liberal theology—the belief that it really doesn't matter what Christ did on the cross so long as we strive to live moral lives. From this perspective, the concept of the Bible as God's divinely inspired revelation can be tossed aside, leaving a view of Scripture as a pleasing, helpful myth.

A RETURN TO PIETISTIC FAITH

Now we can talk about the primary personalities of this chapter—for they all lived and made their contributions to church history in the face of this much-changed world. They spoke as outsiders, rebels against the prevailing worldview of western society. They brought something reborn, yet they were regarded (as believing Christians have been ever since) as intellectual rednecks, old-fashioned thumpers of an outdated book without intellectual relevance. Sound familiar? Their responses weren't reactions to deism, nor even to Kant's humanistic empirical rationalism (Say *that* three times! Actually, it sums up the worldview held by many non-Christians you'll meet, whether they know these words or not). The reactions of these Christian saints were basic faith responses, born out of study of the New Testament church and an attempt to return to what the Bible reveals about its workings. The key to this new understanding was, quite simply, faith.

In the late 1600s, Philip Spener and August Hermann Francke founded what is called *pietism*. They didn't try to be pious in the sense of hyperreligious or rigidly moralistic. Rather, they believed God and sought to live by faith inwardly (through personal devotion to Christ) as well as outwardly (through treating daily life as the arena for faithful living). They thought the state-run Lutheran Church was failing to lead Germans to do anything more than go through the motions of religion. They taught their views and practices to their students. Lutheran leaders accused them of trying to divide the church, when in fact they were only trying to revive it. Francke was driven from one university to another until he settled at Halle, where his life and teaching influenced a young nobleman named Nikolaus Ludwig, Count von Zinzendorf.

MORAVIANS

If the University of Halle was the rallying point for pietism, it was Count von Zinzendorf's lands near Dresden, Germany, that became the staging grounds for the movement's launch into the world. While the philosophers spoke of freedom of thought and tolerance of belief, the kings and princes of Europe did not agree with them. That principle of there being one church in a region (summarized as "whose region, his religion") meant that those who did not hold the accepted religious views of the local prince experienced great persecution.

In 1722 Count von Zinzendorf established a community on his vast lands called Herrnhut (literally, "The Lord's Watch") and invited refugees from persecutions to live there. They came. Von Zinzendorf resigned from the German civil service in 1727 to become the pastor of the group, and in that same year the community experienced a great movement of the Holy Spirit. We might call it a revival today — it certainly matched the description of other revivals in Christian history — and the result was an explosion of evangelistic missionary effort.

It could be said that pietism plus revival results in missions. During this period more missionaries went from that Moravian community to the world than from all other Protestant churches *combined*. They went to the West Indies, to North America (we'll meet those when we talk about Wesley), to Egypt, to Greenland, to South Africa — then to closer places like Holland and England — in each place seeking to share the orthodox faith in Christ Jesus as atoning Lord and Savior.

Count von Zinzendorf was accused (again, by the Lutheran Church of the time) of seeking to start a new church, so he became a Lutheran minister. They booted him out, however, and eventually the Moravian church was organized as a separate communion and continued about its business. Von Zinzendorf was a genuine ecumenical in his relationship to other churches, but not as we understand ecumenism today. He was more like the leaders of the emerging evangelical coalition among churches today. His was a religion of the heart, and anyone who shared it was his brother or sister in

Christ. Denominationalism was not his concern.

It was in this spirit that he welcomed John Wesley to the Herrnhut community. Wesley was pulling together what would become one of the greatest Christian reformation movements in history.

JOHN WESLEY
1703–1791

The organizer of the Methodist movement within the Church of England, John Wesley unintentionally established the Methodist Church. With his brother Charles, a great writer of hymns, Wesley helped revolutionize the spiritual thinking of much of the English population and in the American colonies as well. The Oxford-educated son of an Anglican minister, Wesley spent several years in the Americas as a missionary to Native Americans in Georgia. It was not until later, however, during his "Aldersgate experience," that Wesley came to understand the message of personal conversion that he would preach so effectively for the remainder of his life.

METHODISTS

Early in the 1700s, a son was born to the pastor of an Anglican church in England. His name was John Wesley. Almost as soon as he could walk he was taught to read the Bible, and he was given a very strict and spiritual upbringing, as is often the case with preachers' children. His father was a correct Anglican, but his mother came from a family of Separatists. Susanna Wesley, like Augustine's mother, Monica, poured her heart into the lives of her children.

When John was five years old, the rectory they were living in burned down, and he was the last person to be rescued from the flames. He thought himself to be "a brand plucked from the burning" by God for some special purpose. But although he knew plenty about the Scriptures and lived a moral life, something was missing.

As he grew older, John Wesley followed his father's example into preparation for the ministry at Oxford University. His brother Charles, four years younger, went to Oxford as well, and while John was away from school, Charles started a group there called the Holy Club. When he returned to school, John became its leader and directed the group with disciplined regularity toward Scripture study and prayer. He was trying his best to lead a godly life through the "method" of self-discipline. Other more worldly students at the university scoffed at the group and began to call it the "Methodists." Still—something was missing.

In 1735 John and Charles crossed the Atlantic to the new colony of Georgia. Charles was to be an assistant to the governor, and John was to be a missionary to the Native Americans. The crossing was hard, and both were terrified during a storm, but there was a group of Moravian missionaries sailing with them who viewed their terrifying situation with great faith and calm. John was impressed.

Their two and a half years in Georgia didn't go well for either of the Wesleys. John wasn't a successful missionary, and he became involved with a young lady who broke his heart. When she refused to marry him, he misused his position and refused to give her Communion (talk about a woman scorned?). This naturally caused trouble. Charles, meanwhile, fought with the governor and returned home. John followed him, but only after a long conversation with yet another Moravian missionary, Peter Bohler, who asked if John had Jesus "in his heart." Wesley didn't understand what he was talking about.

Back in England in 1738, Charles had a transforming experience of personal spiritual conversion. Two days later John went to a Christian meeting in Aldersgate Street, London, where he heard Martin Luther's preface to the book of Romans being read. John wrote later that his "heart was strangely warmed." Through all of his spiritual labors, he had felt righteous but unsatisfied and insecure in God. Now he felt that same grace that Luther had discovered. Not long afterward, he preached a sermon on salvation by faith in Christ. This became the theme he emphasized for the next fifty years.

He traveled to Herrnhut and studied for a time what the Moravians were doing. When he returned to England, he maintained his own theological perspectives, but he also had a new model of what a church could and should be. He began to organize—and John Wesley had a gift for organization.

Wesley was Arminian. This meant that he followed the beliefs of Jacob Arminius over those of John Calvin, believing that an individual can, by his or her free will, accept Christ's sacrifice. He believed we can resist the grace of God if we choose. This view also held a higher regard for innate human goodness than Calvin's did—a viewpoint popular during this time. Wesley believed that Christ's death atoned for all who would *accept* it, and that God had elected from the beginning those whom he *foreknew* would do so. As we noted before, in 1619 the Council of Dort had rejected these views as unscriptural, but councils didn't carry the weight with Protestants that the early church councils had carried with Catholics. Wesley's embrace of Arminius's views reanimated this great Protestant controversy, which continues to the present.

Wesley was faithful to the Church of England all his life. He had no intention of becoming a Separatist or starting a new denomination. He simply wanted to plant "Methodist" groups or "Holy bands" in each Anglican church as a means of reforming it. But much as the Lutherans sought to shut out the Moravians in Germany, concerned Anglican clergymen shut these new groups out of churches. So Methodist groups became separate congregations, then built their own Methodist chapels, and gradually pulled away from the Anglican communion and coalesced into a new denomination.

While Wesley struggled to hold the movement within the state Church of England, he *did* ordain two bishops to lead the Methodist movement that was quickly growing in the American colonies—something we'll look at more carefully in the next chapter. In the run-up to the American Revolution, identification with the Church of England had a negative effect on the gospel's advancement in the colonies, so Methodists in America were clearly separated from Anglicans. When Wesley died in 1791, the Methodist Church in America and England had about 175,000 members and over six hundred lay preachers, all of whom were focusing on salvation through faith in Christ alone. Like many of the other personalities we've discussed, John Wesley didn't set out to start a revolution, but he did anyway.

WILLIAM CAREY

In the year after Wesley died, a part-time Baptist preacher in London offered a challenge to his older pastoral colleagues that *was* intentional—and it helped to launch a revolution in the way that Protestant Christians regarded the needs of the world.

His name was William Carey, and although the Moravian missionaries had already been going around the world in Jesus' name for a generation and Jesuits for many generations, his challenge was so direct and piercing that he is known as the father of the modern missionary movement.

WILLIAM CAREY
1761–1834

Carey was an English Baptist who wrote "An Inquiry into the Obligation of Christians to Use Means for the Conversion of the Heathens," arguing that the Great Commission still applied to all Christians. Carey helped to organize the Baptist Missionary Society, then took his family to India in 1793. He spent the remainder of his life at Serampore, near Calcutta, directing missions efforts of various kinds with great success. His methodology became widely imitated, and his example challenged many others to go as missionaries.

Carey was born near Northampton to a poor but well-educated family. His father was the schoolmaster and town clerk, and Carey learned early of faraway lands and distant times. He was apprenticed at twelve as a cobbler, or shoemaker. While he had already been confirmed as a member of the Church of England, he had a conversion experience at eighteen as a result of a fellow apprentice's witness and became a "dissenter"—a Baptist. He was baptized as a believer in 1783 and soon was doing lay preaching. Three years later, he became pastor of a Baptist church in Moulton, then of a church in Leicester, and then he wrote the treatise that would change his life—and the lives of millions.

Carey was greatly influenced by the writings of Jonathan Edwards, the great Calvinist who had been a leader in the American Great Awakening. (We'll get to this in the next chapter.) He'd also been inspired by the story of David Brainerd, Edwards' almost son-in-law who burned himself out as a missionary to the Native Americans in 1746. Following Edwards (and *not* Wesley), Carey was a Calvinist. He was also one of the greatest of missionaries, which certainly counters the argument that Calvinism can't be missionary-minded. Indeed, Edwards' writings had directed Carey *toward* missions.

However, some of Carey's Calvinist Baptist colleagues were hyper-Calvinist in their perspectives. When Carey presented "An Inquiry into the Obligation of Christians to Use Means for the Conversion of the Heathens" to the meeting of his Baptist association, one of his mentors snapped, "Sit down, Carey. If God wants to save the heathen, he can do so without your help."

But the point of the tract was this: We are the means God intends to use to save the world, and the New Testament makes that abundantly clear. Eventually Carey won his colleagues over, and together they organized the Baptist Mission Society—the first of many mission societies in Europe and England that were to scatter missionaries and the seed of the gospel around the world. Carey himself was the first missionary of the society. He went to India—and didn't come back.

Carey's story is not filled with triumph alone. It was seven years before he baptized his first convert. He buried his wife and many of his children in India. But he didn't abandon what he had begun. He expressed a missions philosophy that continues to influence missionaries today. Some of his philosophy is so basic to today's missionary philosophy that you might say, "Well, duh!"

For example, he argued that there should be widespread preaching of the gospel. The fact is, however, that this had *not* been generally practiced in non-Christian lands. He also felt the need to study Indian culture carefully so that he wouldn't make poor judgments about what the Indians were and were not thinking and teaching. This understanding led him to learn and use the local language. He believed in distributing the Bible in local languages, and he made translations to fill this need. He saw that India needed a truly *national* church, one led by trained Indian pastors. Missiologists call this the indigenous principle, the first principle of effective missionary church planting today. The need for trained national pastors moved Carey to establish the Serampore College. In these and other ways, Carey proved himself the chief innovator of modern missions, if not truly its father.

As a result of his example and writings, there soon came a flood of missionaries to aid Carey in lands adjoining India and across the seas. Many of these came from England, while others came from the former colonies — now the United States of America. What had happened in that place to make it one of the primary missions-sending nations? This is where we need to turn our attention next.

First, though — what did this period contribute to our understanding of our six themes?

People Like Us

The people of the eighteenth century, Christians and skeptics alike, were people like us. John Wesley refused Communion to the Georgia peach who rejected him. Carey has been criticized for taking his wife to India, where she first went out of her mind and then died. On the other hand, Carey and Wesley, Spener and Von Zinzendorf, all the Christians we've cited in this chapter, were struggling just as we do with the daily frustrations and temptations of real life. They were people like us—and yet they changed the world through their faithfulness. Some of their changes were unintentional, but God used them nonetheless.

The Body of Christ and the Human Institution

Nonconformists like Wesley's grandparents made clear their insistence that the true church must prove faithful to Christ, whether or not it remains faithful to a king or a hierarchy. As a dissenter, William Carey called for a step that renewed the commitment of the worldwide church to missions. If the human institution of the church was still in evidence—and it was—so too were churches determined to reform that institution to function as the body of Christ. As always, the struggle continued, just as it does today.

Faith Versus Reason

This was the age of reason, and the age used reason to rule God out of daily control of the world. In response, many believers took a stand against cold logic and upon faith. Eventually even the philosophers—especially Kant—concluded that they could say nothing about God based on logic and sensory data alone, and faith continued to stand, unchanged, as the means of access to the God that reason couldn't reach.

We live in a postmodern age that mistrusts science—having seen its failures—and questions logic. Faith—the faith of Catholic Pascal and Moravian von Zinzendorf and

Anglican-Methodist Wesley—remains our means of access to the God who not only created us but seeks to have fellowship with his creation.

Church + State = Very Bad Things

While the state's control over the church remained in place, the arena in which the state felt the need to prove its power had shifted away from religious dissension and to revolutionary politics. By 1800 there were still places where Christians who held a different viewpoint from their sovereign were persecuted, but this was also an age when philosophers were emphasizing tolerance and people were listening. Besides, there was a proven solution to the problem of persecution: emigration to one of the colonies. This option was taken often enough by immigrants to North America that it permanently affected the politics of the American colonies—with obvious results.

What About Missions?

This became the age when missions were placed again among the church's priorities. From this point on, missions spread out around the globe. That worldwide movement continues to expand.

Ethics Optional?

Pietism reasserted the importance of ethical *living* as well as ethical *talking*. The free church movement invested local churches with the power to admit or reject those whose Christian lives they could witness, and church discipline became less the control of church members by priests or leaders and more the control of all by all. The rising demand for ethical living was to make an even greater impact on the next generation of Christians in Europe and America, but we need to see how the faith came to America before we explore that expansion of grace into ethical behavior.

WANT TO KNOW MORE?

There is plenty more to know about this period—a lifetime of learning, actually. But here are some starting places: *Austin's Topical History of Christianity* (Carol Stream, IL: Tyndale, 1983) has been particularly helpful in assembling this chapter. So, too, have been the writings of some of the principal figures themselves—the works of Descartes, Spinoza, Pascal, Newton, Locke, Hume, and Kant. Bertrand Russell's *History of Western Philosophy* (New York: Simon and Schuster, 1945) is an extremely readable introduction to the Enlightenment but is also extremely biased (did you know Enlightenment thinkers liberated the world from barbaric superstition and ushered in a golden age?).

Also available are the collected works of John Wesley and the famous missionary challenge of William Carey, "An Inquiry into the Obligation of Christians to Use Means for the Conversion of the Heathens." Each of these works has exerted enormous influence on the church today, and all are well worth the time it takes to read them.

11

Awakening Faith, Awakening Conscience

REVIVALISM, MILLERISM, AND CHRISTIAN ACTIVISM

The Enlightenment, Pietism, Methodism, missions—all of these movements influenced the New World. But influences from the American colonies had equally powerful effects on the Old World. America was a land of refuge from political and religious oppression for 150 years before uniting as a nation in 1776, and many different Christian perspectives were reflected there. Separatists in New England became Congregationalist Puritans. The tiny colony of Rhode Island gave Baptists freedom from Puritan repression. New York, originally colonized by the Dutch and named New Amsterdam, had its share of Dutch Reformed churches. Pennsylvania was a haven for Quakers. Maryland began as a Catholic colony. In Virginia and the Carolinas the Anglican Church was a mainstay. But in all the colonies, deism and the writings of John Locke and others were popular.

The outcome of all of this was a political experiment called the United States of America. But several things happened that helped bind the colonies together and move them toward inter-action with one another, and one of those things was a Christian movement. It was called the Great Awakening, and it deserves the name. It changed the American church forever, and that change continues to echo both here and across the oceans.

THE GREAT AWAKENING

Propaganda of my first grade teacher to the contrary, the colonies were not all settled by freedom-loving Pilgrims. Many different motives drove people to the colonies, with making money certainly one of the foremost. While both prosperity and freedom were highly valued, social problems abounded — as happens whenever diverse peoples cluster together.

Many of these problems sound familiar: alcoholism, moral laxity among young people, tepid faith in many churches. There were other problems as well: The treatment of Native Americans had produced wars and massacres, and in the South especially the enslavement of workers became more pronounced and institutionalized. These were mostly European-born bond-slaves at first, but gradually the importing of captive Africans became the rule. The colonies may have been lands of promise, but they were lands of compromise as well, and some of these compromises would have terrible consequences.

As in Europe, some in America saw the churches' failure and prayed for a return to New Testament faith. Among these were William Tennent, who founded the log college that even-tually became Princeton University, and Theodorus Jacobus Frelinghuysen, a Dutch Reformed pastor in New Jersey who had been touched by pietism in his homeland. Frelinghuysen preached passionately the need for a reformation of spirit in what he saw as the dead churches of New Jersey. Other pastors complained about him to his superiors in Holland, accusing him of trying to divide the church.

(You'll have noted a pattern by now: People seeking to renew/change the church are often attacked for trying to divide the body or corrupt orthodox doctrine and practice. Traditionalists/conservatives often balk at the suggestion that their churches are dead or backward. A movement that some see as renewal or progress, others see as revisionist, irreverent, or even heretical. We need standards by which to evaluate renewal/progressive movements in the past and in our own day. Does the movement—new or old—uphold the faith as taught by the apostles, or does it disregard or seek to revise key elements? Do the lives of the movement's adherents reflect the Holy Spirit's fruit: love for God, one another, and outsiders; joy; moral integrity; and so on? Where is the renewers' arrogance or the conservatives' arrogance getting in the way of what God wants to do?)

Frelinghuysen was censured for doctrinal error and improper practices, when primarily he was just preaching evangelism, the need for genuine conversion to faith in Christ Jesus, and church discipline. He also encouraged laypersons to preach and to form small groups for Bible study and prayer. His message and methods influenced Gilbert Tennent, William's son, who was his father's student in the Presbyterian pastoral ministry.

William Tennent stirred Presbyterian congregations of New Jersey to reform their faith and practice. He had a passion for evangelism that provoked opposition from his fellow ministers—especially when he preached a sermon called "On the Dangers of an Unconverted Ministry." The title itself was enough to set some pastors' teeth on edge—but it was true. Tennent became one of the great evangelists of the Awakening.

But by far the best-known name attached to the First Great Awakening was that of a hard-line Calvinist theologian named Jonathan Edwards.

JONATHAN EDWARDS
1703–1758

A preacher's son who graduated from the college that would become Yale University, Jonathan Edwards was a brilliant child prodigy who was writing sophisticated theological speculation at the age of fifteen. Initially a Presbyterian Calvinist, he became pastor of the Congregational church at Northampton, Massachusetts. In 1735 a revival began in Northampton that swept up and down the American colonies as the Great Awakening. Known today for his sermon "Sinners in the Hands of an Angry God," Edwards carefully documented the Holy Spirit's movement in Northampton. His church dismissed him in 1750 for refusing to give the Lord's Supper to nonmembers, so he moved to Stockbridge and began preaching to the Native Americans. He was summoned to become president of the College of New Jersey (Princeton) and reluctantly took the post, but died soon after.

JONATHAN EDWARDS AND GEORGE WHITEFIELD

Jonathan Edwards was a Congregationalist preacher's son from Connecticut. He was a brilliant child who mastered Hebrew,

Greek, and Latin by the age of thirteen. By sixteen he had written a philosophy of being in answer to John Locke. At seventeen he graduated at the head of his class, and he became a senior tutor at Yale at twenty-one. Three years later he had a personal experience of spiritual change and commitment to God. He became associate pastor of the Northampton Congregational Church. (In that same year, 1727, Count von Zinzendorf became pastor of the Moravian group at Herrnhut.)

Edwards was not the emotional preacher we tend to associate with evangelistic outpourings today. He was a hard-line Calvinist whose description of the sovereign God has been faulted for lacking mercy. When he dryly read his sermon "Sinners in the Hands of an Angry God," people fainted in terror. But under his leadership the church responded with genuine, heartfelt prayer—and something remarkable began to happen in 1735. Perhaps it was Edwards' reputation for intellectual brilliance and stone-solid views on predestination that validated the events in Northampton as a genuine movement of the Holy Spirit. In 1739 he described it in great detail in *A Faithful Narrative of the Surprising Work of God*. Here he used the term *great awakening*, and the name stuck as the revival spread.

This was a time of great spiritual activity in many places. In the year the revival started in Northampton, John Wesley and his brother Charles came to America. In the year before Edwards published his *Narrative*, Wesley had his Aldersgate experience. Two years later, George Whitefield, an actor turned preacher, arrived in America from England to begin his second preaching tour, and when he preached his way through the colonies, the fires of revival were lit everywhere.

Whitefield had good lungs—perhaps from his theatrical training—and when he was denied the use of a church building, he found he could address up to 25,000 people outside. Revival—a life-changing movement of the Holy Spirit through the preaching of the gospel—came not only to Congregationalist and Presbyterian churches but to many other groups and to the colonies in general. Baptist congregations embraced revivalism to the point that it remains part of the fabric of the denomination today.

Recognizing that association with Anglican churches was unpopular in America, John Wesley ordained Thomas Coke and Francis Asbury as Methodist bishops in the New World, and Methodist churches were planted and began to grow. The Awakening was so pervasive and so cross-denominational that it served a political as well as spiritual end: It helped to unite the diverse American colonies in a common experience. People from the North became known to people in Virginia, and vice versa. While those who gathered in 1776 to sign the Declaration of Independence were not all Christians, they had all been influenced, however indirectly, by the coming of spiritual freedom to North America.

As Whitefield preached, Edwards fed the flames with his writings. In addition to the *Narrative*, he published *A Treatise Concerning Religious Affections* and *Distinguishing Marks of a Work of the Spirit of God*. He also published the journal of David Brainerd, his would-be son-in-law who died after a brief mission to the American Indians in 1741–1742. As for the Northampton church, the revival faded—so much so that Edwards lost his position in a dispute about what it meant to be a member of the church and who could take Communion. He moved to Stockbridge, Massachusetts, and tried to minister to both the white church and an American Indian mission—doubtless inspired by Brainerd's ministry. While in Stockbridge, Edwards wrote his most impressive work, *The Freedom of the Will*, which basically said that man has *no* free will at all with regard to choosing to respond to God. It was a restatement of Calvinist theology written in the terms of the Enlightenment—and in answer to it.

Jonathan Edwards was invited to become president of the "Log College" (Princeton) established by William Tennent. He took the post but died in that same year from a smallpox vaccination gone wrong. The legacy he left behind, however, was enormous. Perhaps one of the most remarkable miracles of the First Great Awakening was that God generated a true movement of the Holy Spirit out of the preaching of a Calvinist who out-Calvined Calvin. Those who decry Calvinism as destructive of missions should understand that many of the greatest of missionary leaders were, like Edwards, Calvinist.

THE SECOND GREAT AWAKENING

Between 1800 and 1830 another Awakening spread through the new United States, particularly in the South and along the western frontier. Methodist and Baptist churches in particular expanded rapidly through the camp meeting approach. People in sparsely settled regions gathered in great encampments that lasted for several weeks. These meetings strengthened relationships in these areas and were often multidenominational, with several different styles of preaching taking place in different parts of the camp. The Cumberland Presbyterians and the Disciples of Christ developed out of this second Awakening. The Methodist bishop Francis Asbury established the pattern of the circuit-riding preacher, traveling thousands of miles in his lifetime, establishing and strengthening Methodist congregations.

There was an indirect theological shift throughout this revival—a movement from Calvinist to Arminian theology. The emphasis in these camp meetings was often placed on the free will of an individual to choose Christ's offer of salvation or to refuse it. From the Calvinist perspective, this sounded like a salvation of works rather than grace—the work being the individual's choice. After early participation in the camp meeting approach, Presbyterians abandoned it, questioning the emotionalism and the lack of doctrinal teaching. As a result, the Methodists and Baptists became the dominant churches in the South and West, and a pattern of thinking was established that eventually led to Pentecostalism.

Another movement arose during this period that has powerfully affected American religion: In 1830, a young man named Joseph Smith established a sect that has come to be known as Mormonism. You've probably heard of Mormonism, but you probably haven't heard of another movement, Millerism, that began around the same time and continues to heavily influence evangelical churches.

MILLERISM AND DISPENSATIONALISM

Ever since the Montanists in the 200s, various Christian groups have been so certain that Christ's second coming is about to occur that they have set the actual date of his appearing. When the first Christian millennium ended in AD 1000, a great spiritual dread came over much of Europe, but Christ didn't return. Again and again, prophets announced the end of the world, but none were correct. By the time of the Second Great Awakening, the predominant view of the Second Coming was what is called *postmillennial*—that is, that Christ will return only after a thousand-year expansion of the church throughout the world. Perhaps this was a natural result of Christianity's apparent victory in all parts of the world during the European colonial era.

But a young Baptist hero of the War of 1812 didn't find postmillennialism convincing. William Miller had just reestablished his faith in Christ Jesus after a flirtation with deism. He was uneducated but felt he could clearly read and understand his Bible, and he began an in-depth study of Bible prophecy. It led him to conclude that Christ would definitely return within twenty-five years. Christ's thousand-year reign would then begin — a view now called *premillennialism*.

Why was Miller so sure? He was convinced that he had found the interpretive key to unlock the Bible's predictive chronology. He wasn't the first to conclude this, nor the last, but his belief may have had the greatest historical influence on the millennial views of Christians today. He didn't immediately share his view, but by 1832 he was writing articles that fixed the date of Christ's return in 1843, and by 1835 he was preaching it publicly.

Between 50,000 and 500,000 Americans from all denominations became convinced that he was correct and made plans to close their earthly affairs. Many preachers rallied to his cause and amplified the message, while many others rejected it and him, closing their pulpits to him and warning their congregations to avoid this new fanaticism. When various denominations put the "Millerites" out of their camp, a new denomination drew together under the name Adventists. (The word *advent* means "coming.") Leading up to 1843, vast tabernacles were built to house believers in the message. But when the chosen year came — and went — and Christ did not return, the great expectation came to be called "the great disappointment."

Miller was devastated. When one of his followers announced that he'd found the problem—a discrepancy in the way that the Jews dated months—Miller felt new hope, and the new date was fixed in 1844. When that date too proved wrong, Miller retired from public life and died a few years later, a disappointed man.

But his teaching lived on. Within a few months of the second failed date, the Seventh-day Adventist Church was formed, putting a different spin on the interpretation of Christ's coming. Also influenced was a young man named Charles Taze Russell, who got into the date-setting business himself as he launched the group we know as Jehovah's Witnesses.

Growing side-by-side with this new focus on the millennium were the teachings of J. N. Darby, a member of the Plymouth Brethren who believed the Bible revealed that God had dealt with mankind in distinct, separate dispensations—and that the dispensation of the church was drawing to an end. When this view of God's relationship to the church was woven together with the vestiges of Millerism, a new form of chiliasm (remember that word?) came to be called *premillennial dispensationalism.*

This view was later amplified through the preaching of Dwight L. Moody and through the Scofield Bible, which imbedded this view into its study notes in a way that seemed to make the notes as inerrant as the Scriptures themselves. Because the Scofield Bible became the primary King James Version used by independent evangelicals and many Baptists, dispensationalism—which wasn't present in church history until the 1800s—remains widely accepted among evangelicals and Pentecostals today.

You may hold this view yourself. Does knowing how

recently it has developed cause you discomfort? This doesn't mean the view is wrong—just that it is recent and that we really don't know exactly how and when the Lord will return. But Jesus told his disciples that it wasn't for them to know the time that the Father has fixed. Should we expect to know more than they? We just know—as has every generation of Christians since Christ ascended—that his return could be any day, and that we need to be at work at the task we've been assigned until he comes.

CHRISTIAN ACTIVISM

Kenneth Scott Latourette gave three volumes of his seven-volume *History of the Expansion of the Christian Church* to the 1800s, calling it the Great Century. Already in this chapter we've seen the explosion of the Second Great Awakening and the renewal of chiliasm (millennialism) as parts of that expansion. During this period, the renewed focus on world missions launched by the pietists and William Carey wrapped the gospel all the way around the world. But there was another powerful renewal taking place within parts, at least, of the church. It was a rediscovery of the ethical obligations of the Christian faith.

Perhaps this was yet another Christian reaction to the Enlightenment. That philosophy had, after all, stripped the supernatural aspects away from religion and identified it as primarily a moral code. Christians living in an Enlightenment-dominated world were forced to reexamine the ethical failures of the church, and they were many. Poverty, slums, drug use, slavery—these scars on the new industrialized economies were obvious. Obvious too was the indirect—or in some cases very direct—support of some churches for these practices. Would

Christians recognize their complicity in these social evils and act to change them?

WILLIAM WILBERFORCE
1759–1833

Born to a wealthy family and well educated, Wilberforce was elected to England's Parliament at age twenty-one. He took with him to government a strong Christian heritage, having been influenced toward evangelicalism by his aunt. He built a strong relationship with William Pitt the Younger, who became prime minister, and he served a model career in Parliament. No one was more regular in attendance or served on more committees. His zeal for moral reform caused him to become involved early in the abolition of the slave trade in the British Empire, a goal to which he devoted his life. He also helped form the Church Missionary Society, the Society for the Suppression of Vice, the Society for the Prevention of Cruelty to Animals, and a bill to outlaw the lottery. Through his efforts, participation in the slave trade by British citizens was banned in 1807, and a month after his death slavery was abolished throughout the British Empire.

When William Wilberforce was born in 1759, the American colonies were still aflame with the Great Awakening, and George Whitefield and John Wesley were changing the religious face of England through their preaching. When his father died, William went to live in London with his uncle and his Aunt Hannah, who was a great supporter of Whitefield. Fifteen-year-old William was impressionable—so much so that his mother and grandfather brought him home to Yorkshire when he was seventeen to get him away from that influence. While evangelicals were mostly Calvinist members of the Church of England, Whitefield's close relationship with Wesley made his views sound too much like Methodism. William went on to attend Cambridge, where he enjoyed social life more than studies. He was a slight, sickly young man, but—although shocked by some students' behavior—he avidly pursued hedonistic pleasure.

His family's fortune had been built on the Baltic trade, but William wasn't much interested in that. Instead he directed his attentions toward politics. As the son of a two-time mayor of Hull, he won election and began his lifelong career in Parliament. This was in 1780, so he was present as votes were taken regarding the war with the colonies and at the time of England's defeat.

He went to France a year later and experienced a spiritual renewal. He began reading his Bible and keeping a journal, and committed himself to giving his life in service to God. When he returned to London, he asked the advice of John Newton, the former slave-trader who wrote "Amazing Grace." By then Newton was the leading evangelical Anglican clergyman, and Wilberforce asked him what he should do. Newton (and others) advised him to stay in politics—and he listened. Perhaps his name is not as well known as those of other English statesmen, but his influence for Christ in a critical time of the empire was immense.

He built a relationship early with William Pitt the Younger, who became prime minister in the aftermath of the British defeat by the United States of America. Like most English leaders, Wilberforce must have felt scarred by this defeat, for as the voices for revolution grew across the channel in France, he helped to found the Society for the Suppression of Vice. Included in the "vices" he wanted to suppress were Thomas Paine's inflammatory writings about liberty in America.

Already Wilberforce was known in Parliament for his position on the slave trade: His first speech against it was in 1789, nearly two years after he helped to form the Committee for the Abolition of the Slave Trade, the cause for which he is best known.

A group of evangelical members of Parliament lived near Wilberforce in Clapham, a part of London. They met together for prayer and worked together in Parliament to seek changes in the law. Called the Clapham Sect or the "Saints" by other members of Parliament, they exerted such fervent continuing pressure toward that goal that they achieved more moral change in England in thirty years than anyone else had made in English history. Central to this change was Wilberforce, who came to be regarded as the nation's conscience. James Boswell described watching Wilberforce address Parliament by saying he looked like a shrimp when he stood up, but he grew throughout the speech until he became a whale.

Through the war with revolutionary France, through the second war with the United States, through the battle with Napoleon, Wilberforce was present to make his beliefs known. In 1797 he completed *A Practical View of the Prevailing Religious System of Professed Christians*, in which he called on all Christians to recognize the obligations of the Christian faith. He spoke of what he called the "peculiar doctrines" of the faith that created a passion for goodness and morality. But he wasn't writing merely an ethical system. He believed that the grace of God and the sacrifice of Christ, when fully understood, would change the nation. His book was a bestseller, was translated into five languages, and changed lives. And while he was often attacked, called a hypocrite by some, and physically threatened, he held to his course. The personal cost was high.

He was always sickly. His doctors prescribed a new wonder drug to help him, without being fully aware of its power or its side effects, and he became addicted to opium. This didn't bear the stigma it does today, but the result was gradual morphine poisoning that affected his eyes and caused him fearful hallucinations. Through it all, he maintained his commitment to God and to his task, and was instrumental in starting dozens of organizations to deal with moral ills. But he wasn't a pragmatist, the person who says "we should be moral because it's good for society." He was a Christian. He did good because he loved God and was compelled by his worship of God's majesty and glory.

He died in 1833 with the final victory over slavery in the British Empire in view, and he rejoiced. This exerted massive political, financial, and spiritual pressure on the United States, where the "evil institution" persisted for another generation and nearly broke the young nation apart. Still, it was Wilberforce's example of living out one's Christian convictions in political life that advanced this cause—and many others—into the world's conscience. Harriet Beecher Stowe mentioned his influence in *Uncle Tom's Cabin*, the book which, more than any other single influence, pushed many American Christians to fight for the abolition of slavery. John Newton had been right: God had set aside Wilberforce for a great task.

There are so many more heroes of the faith during this period than we can describe individually, but their contributions were great and the world is not worthy of them. What of Whitefield, Asbury, Finney, Moody, Spurgeon, Scofield? The list could go on and on. The 1700s and 1800s were filled with men and women of faith who acted on their convictions and made a difference. We can't touch them all—much less all the greats of the twentieth century.

Before we get to the twentieth century, let's think of how our themes played out in the 1700s and 1800s.

People Like Us

Jonathan Edwards, William Miller, William Wilberforce, and all the other people mentioned in this chapter were definitely people like us. Each one of these three was totally convinced of the truth of his cause. Each faced opposition, often from forces within the church. Each experienced failures and disappointments. Although one of America's greatest theologians, Edwards was fired from his church. While he helped Christians to focus once more on the promise of Christ's return, Miller was wrong about the date. Twice. Wilberforce lived as a man after God's own heart, but he was an Englishman of his time and had no qualms about suppressing free speech—especially if it could lead to something as troublesome as the American Revolution. All those and many others who lived by faith and died in faith were merely people. Yet God has chosen to use people to communicate his glory.

The Body of Christ and the Human Institution

This was a period when Christians rediscovered the power of prayer and preaching, and also spoke and wrote much about the failure of dead orthodoxy. Christians challenged one another to not just talk the gospel but to live it. Churches awoke from years of meaningless ritual into fiery conviction. But there was certainly fallout from the revivals that swept

Great Britain and America. One outcome was a proliferation of new denominations—and some cults—each certain that it alone had the truth. The human institution of the church divided and subdivided over a host of smaller and smaller issues, all in search of a return to being the body of Christ on earth, but each revealing in its self-assurance a predictably human pride. On the foreign mission fields these divisions caused great confusion. They still do.

Faith Versus Reason

Jonathan Edwards reacted to Enlightenment questions by reframing Calvin's arguments in new, perhaps harder, ways. Wesley took the Arminian view, rephrasing it into a new system. Both these views were *reasonable* systems. Both were based on interpretations of biblical passages, yet they were opposed to one another. Throughout the 1700s and 1800s, there was constant examination and reexamination of the process and means of justification by faith—what it means to be Christian. Why all this emphasis on reason as opposed to mystery? Why did (do) Christians argue so violently over the right interpretation, when the Scriptures say that God's wisdom confounds the wise? Perhaps because the overwhelming emphasis on human *reason*—the modernism of the Enlightenment—required that kind of response. We'll need to examine in the last chapter whether in our *post*modern age the anti-Enlightenment arguments carry the same weight.

Church + State = Very Bad Things

With Wilberforce in mind, can we still make the statement that the combined power of church and state is always negative? The fact is, Wilberforce didn't seek to compel the British Empire to control people through religion, as many before him had. Instead, he sought to demonstrate the influence of the individual Christian conscience through the political process—and there's a real difference here. Wilberforce demonstrated that speaking, voting, and living one's Christian convictions in a democratic system makes a difference by means of *influence*, rather than through compulsion.

Perhaps he tended to want to force people to do right—that's common to many of us when we see so much wrongness around us. But the system of government would not allow that. Instead he carried on a political ministry through influence, making a much greater lasting difference than those who sought to regulate behavior through the church. His seems to be a much more effective—and New Testament—way of relating to the state. The question now, as it was then, is whether Christians will actually live out their faith though the political process.

What About Missions?

The Great Century of Advance, Latourette called it—the time when the Great Commission again became a current obligation rather than just an ancient suggestion. This was the age of Rufus Anderson and Henry Venn and Hudson Taylor, all worthy of study. Today's global outreach of Christ's body is built on the foundations laid by these and other great missionaries. They made some mistakes in methodology—the "white man's burden" was an inherently racist statement—and many missions became excuses for European paternalism. But God used this flood of missions-minded people to organize, educate, heal, and inspire people of many lands.

Ethics Optional?

For the Christians of this age, the answer to this question became a most emphatic no. The rise of social consciousness—whether focused on Native Americans, orphans, slaves, poverty, morality, alcoholism, gambling, or whatever—demanded that Christians act on their convictions. More, it challenged Christians to examine whether, if they had no such convictions, they were truly Christians. It's still a potent question to ask of Christians today.

WANT TO KNOW MORE?

This chapter only touches on a few people who greatly influenced the American religious scene. Further study on George Whitefield and Francis Asbury would add to a rounded picture of the birth of American Christianity. John Mark Terry's *Evangelism: A Concise History* (Nashville: Broadman & Holman, 1994) is a brief but effective resource. In Richard Abanes' *End-Time Visions: The Doomsday Obsession* (Nashville: Broadman & Holman, 1998) there is a lengthy chapter on William Miller. The magazine *Christianity Today* has a wonderful website linked to capsules on "Christians you should know." And of course, Jonathan Edwards' writings, David Brainerd's journal, Wilberforce's *Practical View*, and Stowe's *Uncle Tom's Cabin* are all available.

12

The Explosive Twentieth Century

LIBERALISM, MASS EVANGELISM, AND PENTECOSTALISM

At the beginning of the twentieth century, there were about 1.5 billion people in the world. After 1950 that population figure had doubled to 3 billion, and by the end of the century had doubled again to 6 billion. During this period, the percentage of evangelical Christians grew from only 2.5 percent of the world's population in 1900 to 11.2 percent by the year 2000. For the first time in world history, there is one committed believer for every nine people in the world.[2]

Of course, such figures are speculative. As Patrick Johnson says, Christian researchers don't have access to the Lamb's Book of Life mentioned in Revelation. Still, the point is that the evangelical Christian presence in the world has exploded over the last century and continues to grow. What happened? Who is responsible for this amazing change?

The answer is, of course, the Holy Spirit. But God has chosen to work through people to make his glory known, so there are people we can identify who have been instrumental in all of this. Many people. Too many to put into a single chapter of this small book.

If you look at a vast, spreading oak you can see clearly the main trunk, grown thick with age. You can see major limbs spreading from the trunk, smaller but still thick and powerful. Then you see one of these major limbs branching into successively smaller branches, spreading out wide and reaching high into the sky. It's an old illustration, but appropriate for our understanding of church history. During the twentieth century, the church — especially the evangelical church — has leafed out. It's easy to tell that Polycarp, Athanasius, and Augustine are part of the trunk of Christian history. It's easy to see how the major branches like Orthodox, Catholic, and Protestant fork off of that sturdy foundation. But later figures who have played key roles in smaller branches get obscured in the leaves, despite being just as influential in the growth of the church.

We can identify a few whos that illuminate the changes of the last century. More valuable, however, might be a look at some whats — some trends over the last hundred years that have brought the church to what we see today. Many of these are wonderful. Some are not, for the twentieth century was explosive in many negative ways as well as positive.

Changes

The twentieth century was a time of revolution around the world, from the communist revolution in Russia to the technological revolution at the end of the century. This was the century of the World Wars and the United Nations. The colonial empires collapsed in the wreckage of World War II, and in the middle of the century new nations arrived on the scene every week. I was a school kid at that time, and it seemed every new *National Scholastic* told of a new nation and new leader whose unpronounceable names we had to memorize.

During that same period, segregation's hold on much of the United States was broken—often with bloodshed. Not only were civil rights at issue, but so were the rights of women in American society. A so-called sexual revolution hammered morals in many nations and continues to do so. The technological revolution continues to make lasting changes as well. While in the 1950s we knew little of the rest of the world besides what we read in *National Geographic*, now we can know instantly what happens in the rest of the world and read a blogger's personal account of the events. The Internet has made it possible for just about anyone anywhere to instantly communicate with anyone anywhere else. The world has changed.

The explosions of population and communication have fueled several other explosions. Knowledge has exploded. There's far too much for any person to know. Wealth has also exploded—at least for some. The polarization between rich and poor is far greater than it has ever been; the rich are richer, and the poor are as poor as ever. The growth in knowledge and communication has produced new ways to make money and a cultural explosion that is in some ways very diverse and in others very homogenized. That is, there is a growing one-world culture with many different cultural shadings. People from many different cultural perspectives have reacted fiercely to the loss of their culture and defended it through laws or war or terrorism. A by-product—or perhaps a driving force—in this cultural explosion has been the eruption of multiple religious and philosophical perspectives.

There was a time in the early 1900s when Christian scholars expected the other major world religions—especially Hinduism, Buddhism, and Islam—to gradually disappear. They were on the defensive around the world because of both missions and colonialism. But they didn't disappear. Instead, these religions have rebounded and have been imported into the formerly Christian countries of Europe and the Americas. This has been largely the result of immigration, but there has also been some conversion of former Christians into these other world systems. The New Age movement blends many viewpoints, but the basics of it are largely Hindu ideas redrafted with a Western perspective. On the edges of all the major world religions have grown up cults of various kinds. Many groups that evangelical Christians call cults were born out of Christianity. Orthodox Muslims regard Baha'i as a cult born out of Islam.

What happened within the church to cause so much change from the time of the Awakenings to the present? To answer that, we have to go back to the continuing effects of the Enlightenment.

Liberalism

From the time the church collected the writings of the apostles and others into the New Testament, it has regarded the Bible as God's Word. While Christians interpreted the Bible in different ways at different times, its truth and authority went unquestioned. But in the late 1800s Bible scholars reacting to Enlightenment rationality took a different approach. As Darwin's theory of the evolution of life became more widely accepted, scholars applied it to the growth of cultures as well. Some said the Bible began as a cultural record of an "evolving" movement—Christianity. They looked at what they knew about the Bible's origins and questioned the historical church's assumptions.

Did Isaiah write all of the book of Isaiah, or was it rather written by two or even three people of different times? How and when did the first five books of the Old Testament come together? Instead of being written by Moses, did they come from four clearly different sources? What about the books of the New Testament? Did the apostles or their close associates write them, or were they written by anonymous Christians of a later time? In this critical onslaught, the Bible lost—for some—its spiritual authority. Many began to see the Bible as purely a human product, devoid of supernatural content. Much of the impetus for this movement came from Germany, but the ideas spread to Britain and the United States. The ideas took strong root in theological seminaries and universities, and the theories were built upon until they came to be regarded as fact. Not for all Christians, of course—not even for a majority—but as these ideas were repeated and accepted by succeeding generations, they changed the ways preachers proclaimed the biblical message to their congregations.

Reaction among many conservative Christians was immediate and sharp. Professors were fired. Churches and denominations split apart. Schools broke away from the denominations that had founded them. Organizations were formed on both sides of what came to be called the liberal-fundamentalist controversy. Scarcely any Christian denomination went untouched by the debate. Missionaries returned home to find that the churches they represented had shifted away from the supernatural faith they had been proclaiming. Many denominations gradually cut their missions force as they stopped believing that the gospel offered a distinctive way to connect to God through Christ Jesus. Why send missionaries to proclaim Christ if you think the religions people are already practicing are just as good?

We need to be careful. It is easy to question a person's writings to assess how their beliefs differ from yours. It is much harder—no, *impossible*—to know the true relationship of another's heart to God. The fact is, however, that in many Christian denominations the gospel took a backseat to a system of morality based on human values rather than Scripture. While that continues in some denominations to the present, in the early twentieth century, in Germany, where liberal theology first flourished, some thinkers began to try to move modern Christian thinking back to orthodoxy. They didn't make it all the way back, and their movement—called *neoorthodoxy* (new orthodoxy)—fell short of a full return to Scripture. But it was a start.

The theologian Karl Barth is often credited as the first voice of this movement. He was pastoring a church in Germany during World War I when he realized that, as he put it, his people had come to church looking for bread, and he was giving them stones. He meant that they were looking for spiritual food and all he could provide was Lutheran dogma that he found lifeless. Did he see on the horizon the horrors of Hitler's Nazi Germany, which sought to make the church an arm of racist hatred and paganism? Soon after Germany's loss in World War I, that terrible movement began to rise. One young theologian who raised his voice against it—and was eventually killed by the Nazis for his adamant opposition to them—was Dietrich Bonhoeffer.

DIETRICH BONHOEFFER
1906–1945

A German Lutheran pastor and theologian, Bonhoeffer took a stand against Nazism that ultimately cost him his life. A founding member of the Confessing Church, an organization formed in resistance to the Nazi takeover of the German church, he was banned from preaching and arrested for teaching young German pastors in opposition to Hitler. He joined a plot by the Abwehr (German Intelligence) to assassinate Hitler, but was caught, arrested, and jailed. He is best known in America for his book *The Cost of Discipleship.* He paid the ultimate cost himself, as the Nazi authorities hanged him a few weeks before the end of World War II.

BONHOEFFER'S DISCIPLESHIP

Dietrich Bonhoeffer grew up in some privilege as the son of a Berlin doctor. He showed early promise as a Christian scholar and theologian, and Karl Barth encouraged him in his pursuit. He was trained at German universities where liberalism had devalued Scripture's authority and undermined the foundational gospel of Christ, and this experience influenced the way he thought and wrote. Nevertheless, his faith in Christ was deep, and his committment to historic Christianity was real. He spent some time in New York at Union Theological Seminary, which proudly claimed its heritage as a liberal seminary. However, he also attended worship services at the Abyssinian Baptist Church in Harlem, where he was deeply moved by African American gospel music.

He returned to Germany in 1931 and saw the damage the growing Nazi movement was doing to the church. He opposed it, becoming one of the founders of what was called "the Confessing Church," which called German Christians back from the hatred and violence of the Nazi movement. Many German Christians joined him, Karl Barth, and others, but Hitler's power was too great to overcome. Bonhoeffer preached until the Nazi government banned him from preaching, then he organized an underground seminary to continue teaching the true faith to young pastors who sought to hold to their faith. The Nazis closed the seminary, but he continued to meet with his students whenever and wherever he could. He spoke up against the Nazi authorities even though he knew he could be arrested for doing so. Indeed, he was arrested and released, but he continued to preach and teach wherever he could.

Hitler tried to absorb the German Lutheran Church into the Nazi movement. Some bishops became Nazi brownshirts, actually wearing the uniform into their pulpits. Hitler chose a supporter named Ludwig Müller as bishop of this new Nazi church. Bonhoeffer saw the Nazis take over the churches, even replacing Bibles in the pews with Hitler's book *Mein Kampf.* He could have left Germany, as many other strong Christians did. He was offered a teaching position at Union Seminary, and even went to America to take it—but he couldn't stay. He couldn't leave Christians and Jews in Germany without an advocate. He returned to the spiritual battle in his nation.

His most famous book remains a classic today: *The Cost of Discipleship.* Published in 1937, shortly before the war, it appealed to Christians to live out their faith in *every* way. Bonhoeffer argued against "cheap grace"—grace from God that didn't result in lives changed and dedication to changing the world. He sought to marry Christian devotion with a social conscience—something evangelical churches had only begun to do fairly recently. This is a *holistic* (think whole-istic) understanding of the faith that reflects the same concern for contemporary circumstances that drove William Wilberforce. Jesus didn't only care for people's spirits. He cared about their whole personal experience. Isn't that the gospel?

When Bonhoeffer became convinced that only by removing Hitler from power could Germany return to the place where it could honor God, he joined a secret organization that was plotting to kill Hitler. He carried messages concerning a plot that almost succeeded—but didn't. With many others, Bonhoeffer was arrested and jailed in 1943. While in prison, he wrote letters to those outside, talking about his prayer life, his thoughts and reflections, his encounters with others, both guards and prisoners, and his faith in God. As Nazi Germany crumbled, he was moved from prison to prison. Finally, just a few weeks before the war ended, he was hanged to death. Still, his writings had influenced many. His *Letters and Papers from Prison* has been particularly meaningful to Christians ever since.

Like John Bunyan, Bonhoeffer never quit preaching or teaching, even when he was imprisoned for his unswerving commitment to spreading the gospel of Christ. Despite his circumstances, he honored God with his witness, and was killed because of it—much like Paul.

Cheap grace is the mortal enemy of our church. Our struggle today is for costly grace.

DIETRICH BONHOEFFER, *THE COST OF DISCIPLESHIP*

EFFECTS OF WORLD WAR II

World War II changed so much about the world that you could almost say it changed everything. The two world wars together led to mass disillusionment with the church in Europe. Before the wars, most Europeans were churchgoers, at least, and many were orthodox in their faith. But the failure of many European Christian leaders to resist the jingoistic militarism of WWI or the fascism and racism of the Nazis made many post-war Europeans turn their backs on Christianity. The state churches of Europe lacked the internal vibrancy to respond effectively to this disillusionment. Europe was de-Christianized.

The war changed the church in the United States as well—but in a very different direction. While the shattered peoples of Europe lost faith, the victorious United States experienced spiritual revivals. Soldiers returning from the war had seen things that had driven them to God, and they led their families to church. In America, the 1950s became a great time of revival in many churches. It was during this period that a young evangelist named Billy Graham began to preach, and we'll turn to him in a moment. Also, many former soldiers returned as missionaries to areas where they had served in the war. As colonialism died, the way was opened for the gospel to spread everywhere.

But another great shift in the church occurred during this period that was also, in part, born out of World War II. Reformation within the Roman Catholic Church led to a watershed council known as Vatican II. The convener of this council was a pope whose life and ministry had been powerfully changed by the war.

POPE JOHN XXIII (ANGELO GIUSEPPE RONCALLI)
1881–1963

The son of Italian sharecroppers, Roncali served as priest and secretary to a bishop before being drafted into the Italian army during World War I. First made a bishop in Bulgaria in 1921, he was sent in 1935 to Turkey and Greece. He used his office to save Jewish refugees from the Nazis — so effectively that some Jews consider him to be a "righteous gentile." His motto was "obedience and peace," and he demonstrated his practical faith to the point that he was elected Pope John XXIII in 1958. Because of his age, he was expected to be a short-term pope, but three months after his election he announced that he would hold a new ecumenical council, now known as Vatican II, and seek to restore unity to the church. He died before the council was completed, but it radically changed the Roman Catholic Church.

While many conservative Catholics criticized the new direction taken by their church, one result of the council was to open up Roman Catholics to the "separated brethren" of other Christian churches (Greek Orthodox, Protestant, and so on) and to the world at large. In many ways, the lengthy ministry of the beloved Pope John Paul II was built on a foundation laid by the Second Vatican Council. While the Roman Catholic Church continues to maintain that it is the fullest expression of the church, many wounds that had remained open since the Protestant Reformation have begun to heal.

MASS EVANGELISM
The globalization of world communications throughout the twentieth century changed the world. Inevitably, it also changed

the church. Today, satellite transmissions of Christian broadcasts can and do go anywhere. But how did the church get to this point? In a way, it's been through the expansion of the revivalism of George Whitefield and other evangelists of his day, who set the pattern for preaching to large groups. Whitefield's theater-trained lungs allowed him to preach to thousands at once. Public address systems made this far easier, and radio and television multiplied that access a thousandfold, then a millionfold. We can see those steps unfolding through the ministry of one of the best known evangelists in history — Billy Graham.

WILLIAM FRANKLIN (BILLY) GRAHAM JR.
1918–

Probably the best known figure among modern evangelical Christians, Billy Graham preached the simple message of gospel conversion through direct crusades and through all forms of media for more than fifty years. His Billy Graham Evangelistic Association pioneered in the use of media as a tool of evangelistic preaching, beginning with radio and moving to the production of television specials, Christian films, and webcasts. He became a spiritual adviser to a succession of U.S. presidents and has held conversations with many other world leaders. Having preached directly to more than 200 million people through crusades and many millions more through media, Billy Graham can be safely said to have preached the gospel to more people than anyone else in history.

Billy Graham grew up on a dairy farm in North Carolina. Raised Presbyterian, he writes that his primary interest as a young man was fast cars, but he attended a Baptist revival meeting and found himself compelled by the message. Although the evangelist, Mordecai Ham, considered the meeting largely a failure because of lack of response, Graham made his profession of faith in that meeting. What an impact that one decision for Christ has made in the world.

While a student at Wheaton College, Graham pastored a church that took over a radio program. He hoped to move into the military chaplaincy, but illness prevented him, and instead he helped to found Youth for Christ.

His ministry as a traveling evangelist began with a tent-meeting revival—what he called a crusade—in Los Angeles in 1949. This crusade followed the pattern of the Billy Sunday sawdust trail revivals, an often imitated method of evangelical meetings. A Circus-type tent would be put up, sawdust thrown on the floor, and the preaching would begin. The Los Angeles crusade caught fire spiritually. Some have credited newspaper magnate William Randolph Hearst for puffing Graham into a national figure, but certainly the Holy Spirit inspired the ministry that unfolded. Graham preached crusades in other major cities, then in other parts of the world, and the ministry continued to expand. He launched a radio program called *The Hour of Decision*, which continues to be broadcast worldwide. In 1956 he helped to found the magazine *Christianity Today*, one of the best-known and most highly regarded Christian publications in the world.

Graham largely avoided politics, although many presidents welcomed him to the White House, and he often prayed with them and offered spiritual advice. In the 1970s, he helped to organize and enable a world evangelism conference in Lausanne, Switzerland, that became a turning-point meeting for world evangelical Christianity. His association pioneered the use of all forms of media as evangelistic tools, from newspaper columns to television specials to Christian films.

Throughout his long ministry, Graham always sought to avoid the problems that had stained the names of other evangelists. His organization developed the Modesto Manifesto in 1948 to govern the group's actions related to money, sexual morality, criticism of local churches, and self-promotion. Graham always took moderate financial compensation and set up policies to guard him against charges of sexual impropriety. This is one of the reasons he remained highly respected, even by those who didn't agree with him.

He had his miscues—his voice was recorded on the Nixon Watergate tapes agreeing with Nixon's vocal anti-Semitism, a mistake for which he later worked hard to apologize to Jewish leaders. Some evangelicals felt he widened his interpretation of God's grace in his later years to make it possible for people to be saved outside Christ. But for the most part his ministry was an unbroken legacy of integrity of character, simplicity of message, and fidelity to Christ.

The tool of mass evangelism that Graham modeled has continued to be used effectively not only in the United States but in many places around the world. What Whitefield did in the Great Awakening continues today in marketplaces in Africa, Latin America, and anywhere local evangelists have the freedom to preach.

PENTECOSTALISM

Many of those marketplace evangelists would call themselves Pentecostals—a term that describes a relatively recent addition to the church's vocabulary. While the movement dates itself to the day of Pentecost, fifty days after Christ's resurrection, most historians trace its launch to the Azusa Street revival in Los Angeles at the beginning of the twentieth century. However, its roots go back further than that—into the 1800s and the ministry of Phoebe Palmer.

Phoebe Palmer was born in 1807 in New York and raised a Methodist. She and her husband studied John Wesley's writings and became focused on his teachings on Christian perfection—that is, on the ability of fully sanctified Christians to live free of sin. Palmer wrote that she had never felt she'd had the proper *feelings* at conversion but that she came to recognize that if she laid her everything upon Christ's altar, he would honor her sacrifice with sanctification, holiness. She is considered the founder of the Holiness Movement, which influenced the Methodist Church, William Booth (founder of the Salvation Army), the Church of the Nazarene, the Christian and Missionary Alliance, the Church of God (Anderson, Indiana), and other denominations wherein Christian perfection is taught. As the Holiness Movement developed in America, especially through camp meetings, it began to emphasize a "Pentecostal baptism of the Holy Ghost."

It was Charles Fox Parham, a Methodist minister who was part of the Holiness Movement, who first preached that glossolalia, or speaking in tongues, was the evidence or sign of this Holy Ghost baptism. True salvation was then a two-step process—redemption through faith in Christ (and sometimes by virtue of water baptism) and sanctification through the filling of the Holy Ghost.

An African-American pastor named William Seymour learned these teachings from Parham, even though he was excluded from Parham's classroom because of his race. Seymour led the Azusa Street revival in Los Angeles, which began in 1906 and continued for several years. Most Pentecostal churches trace their beginnings in some way back to the Azusa Street meeting, although many of these churches divided along racial lines early on and have only recently begun to unite again.

Most American Protestants took little notice of Pentecostalism until the 1960s, when the charismatic movement began to influence Protestant churches along similar lines. The second-blessing or two-step salvation theology ran counter to that of many denominations, and many churches split or were started as a result of these disagreements. But the charismatic movement, which largely remained within denominations instead of beginning new denominations, was more welcome in evangelical circles with the growth of Christian music and the crossover of praise singing into more traditional churches.

Another point of linkage has been a growing political awareness among evangelicals. Groups have begun to speak one another's denominational language, so cooperation in missions and evangelistic crusades has become far more possible. Battles over charismatic and Pentecostal beliefs and practices continue in some places and denominations, but a telling statistic is that about a quarter of the world's Christians today are Pentecostal or charismatic. The largest church in the world is Yoido Full Gospel Church, a Pentecostal church in South Korea, which has over 800,000 members. Some count Pentecostalism as the third force of Christianity, alongside Roman Catholics and Protestants. Pentecostalism is the fastest-growing Christian movement in the world.

So what about our six themes? How can they help us assess the dynamic changes of the twentieth century?

People Like Us

One of this book's goals has been to demonstrate that these figures from the past are people like us. That was certainly clear in the twentieth century as people—sometimes whole national churches—were sidetracked from the gospel of Christ Jesus into humanistic liberalism or racism—even into support of genocide. But throughout the century there were many Christians, churches, and denominations who continued to place Christ Jesus—his life, teachings, and sacrifice—at the forefront. Churches that abandoned the foundation of the Bible have dwindled in membership and influence. Churches that elevated Christ have grown.

There are probably aspects of your own faith that are clearly from God but other aspects of your life that you'd prefer not to share with anyone. The joy of the Christian faith is that by grace God is reconciling us to himself. Sure, you're flawed. So am I. But so were all those who went before us. While your name may never be written down in a book, your life will make a difference in others' lives. Think about the lives of these great saints, and choose to make a contribution to God's kingdom.

The Body of Christ and the Human Institution

In every generation the struggle between the godly body of Christ and the human institution called the church has been waged anew. It's always new for us, for we've never lived before. Just as these people struggled to maintain what Wesley called the "higher" church in the face of the cold rituals of the "lower" church, we need to continue that struggle today. It's spiritual warfare. It's a war that won't cease until Christ comes again—whenever that may be. And if that's not soon, then visualize the inhabitants of the Martian colony in 2100 battling the same problems in church that we do today.

There is no permanent fix for this problem other than

obedience and faith. Any gathering of Christians becomes an institution fairly quickly as the group lays down ways of thinking and doing things. Some Christians today are so frustrated with institutions that they try to practice the faith on their own, but the New Testament faith is impossible to live outside community.

Look back at church history and realize this won't be over until *everything* is over. Deal with it. No, literally, *deal* with it, in your own life, in your own church. If you don't, who will?

Faith Versus Reason

Reason? What's that? In place of the rigid logic of modernism — the Enlightenment's gift to us, with all its problems — we live in the age of nonlogical whatever-you-want-it-to-be-ism. It's called postmodernism because it follows after the logical empiricism of the modern age. A lot of people use the term but few understand it — which is, in a way, a quirky definition of postmodernism.

You see, postmodernism isn't about logic and substance. It's largely about style and perception. In its extreme form there are no absolute truths. Everything is relative. Nobody is right — or wrong, either. It's difficult to do serious thinking with this outlook. Still, postmodernists accurately recognize that we live in a cultural mall, where ideas and viewpoints compete like movie choices at the multiplex cinema, and the individual can pick and choose among them as he or she pleases. The Protestant Reformation defended the individual's right and responsibility to read the Bible, decide what he or she believes, connect directly with God, and live according to that faith. Five centuries later, that breakthrough defense of the individual has become a hyperindividualism where many people think creating their own designer faith is just fine.

If there are no absolute truths—things that are always true, regardless of who says it—then everything is absolutely false. Where did this skepticism about truth come from? To answer that we need to take a more reasoned, *modern* approach and try to work out the influences logically. One is surely the failure of science to solve the world's problems. Also, politics and advertising have so abused the concept of truth that many people mistrust *any* authority that claims to know what is true. The more we know about failures by church leaders, politicians, parents, and other authority figures, the more people are inclined to mistrust authority of any kind. Thus, many people today have given up on the Enlightenment's enormous trust in reason as a guide to truth.

What can we rely on? The current answer is our own personal experience. For many, "faith" no longer means relying on someone (Christ) or something (the writings of his apostles in the Bible and the historic teachings of the church) beyond the self. For many people today faith means believing what I choose to believe, based on my own experience. Intuition and personal encounters are trusted more than logical reasoning or historic teaching. Luther's insight that each individual believer matters because God saves individuals has developed over five centuries into a hyperfocus on ourselves *as* individuals—on individual relationship with God and a faith comprised of an individual's opinions, beliefs, and chosen practices. (We should note that while hyperindividualism and skepticism about truth are pervasive in Europe and North America, the booming churches of Africa, Asia, and Latin America are more comfortable with truth and are highly communal.)

If the Enlightenment and the modern period overemphasized thinking—and they did—then postmodernism has overemphasized feelings. But if the pendulum has swung in the direction of individual experience, we can perhaps hope for more balance as Christians continue to wrestle with what it means to be human — mind *and* body, rational and emotional and experiential, individuals intimately connected to other believers in a community that spans the continents and the centuries.

But one key lesson we need to learn from church history is that we need to address people where they are *today* — not where they aren't or where they should be or where most people were four hundred years ago. A large part of the church today hasn't realized that people aren't listening anymore to rational explanations of the faith and logical presentations of the failures in their thinking. If we want to communicate the faith to people who are postmodern in their thinking, we have to recognize the value our society places on style, on creativity, on perception — on the *personal*.

Fortunately, while the means of sharing the message may change, the message itself remains the same. Many past saints had to learn that the hard way, as the methods of thought and reason shifted beneath them like the floor during a California earthquake. When it comes to sharing your faith, share what you know personally about God and *how* you know it. If you are certain about what you believe and open and engaging in sharing it, others will listen. Despite the casual disregard of absolute truth, people today are really hungry for a foundation.

Church + State = Very Bad Things

The best example of this rule in the twentieth century was Nazi Germany. I hope our look through church history has convinced you that laws, rules, conquests, politics of any kind will not save the world for Christ Jesus. Christians who have found themselves bound to the state through the church have only been forced to struggle to free it again. But didn't Jesus say something about rendering to Caesar things that are Caesar's, and to God the things that are God's? Didn't he say "My kingdom is not of this world"?

Wilberforce and Bonhoeffer came to the same conclusion but ended up on opposite sides of the political authorities in their time and place. That conclusion is, change government to become more Christlike when you can, and when you can't, oppose it with all the influence you can muster. Remember always, however, that there is far more to life and value than what can be influenced in this world.

What About Missions?

If the nineteenth century was the great century of missionary advance, then the twentieth century was the explosive century of missionary dispersion. Yet there are still many areas of the world where Christ is not known. There remain many unreached people groups in the world (and in your neighborhood), waiting without knowing it for someone who is willing to come. Church history tells us that people come to know Jesus as Lord when the church is missional in nature—but that really means when individuals like *you* see the world as in need of Christ. The missionary explosion continues. Will you be a part of it?

Ethics Optional?

There was probably never a time when unethical actions by Christians could be swept under the rug. Still, Christians are tempted to try — to hold Christ in one hand and the world in the other — and they fail and fall. The nearly simultaneous fall of several highly visibile televangelists in the late twentieth century caused wreckage not only to their own reputations but to that of Christ. Part of postmodernist thinking is moral relativism, which leads to the concept of "lifestyle choice," which the Bible describes succinctly as "everyone did what was right in his own eyes" (Judges 17:6). Another word it uses? *Sin*.

The great role models of the twentieth century were people like Billy Graham and Dietrich Bonhoeffer, who believed that right and wrong were both knowable and non-optional. Without rigid legalism, Graham structured his ministry to avoid the moral failings about sex, money, and power that plagued other evangelists. And Bonhoeffer was willing to die opposing the moral flexibility that allowed German churchgoers to tolerate the Holocaust. The hyperfocus on the individual and the reaction against the Enlightenment has led many people to think that each individual gets to decide what is right and wrong for him or her in any given situation. But those whom we recognize as the great Christians of the past century and our own day are people who have the courage to act on ethical commitments.

One essential value that we've seen exhibited over and over in our look at the greats of church history was character. Have you ever considered what *integrity* means? It means held together, united, all one, whole. Jesus wants to make us whole. We'll never make a lasting impression on the world for Christ if we toss our character aside. A moment of weakness is a character flaw. Why even go there? Christians can't afford to — not and remain effective messengers of the gospel.

What Do You Think?

The church continues to spread and to struggle. Other books deal with the present and the potential future, but our goal was to think about church history. So, what do *you* think?

WANT TO KNOW MORE?

The Churching of America (1776–2005): Winners and Losers in Our Religious Economy (New Brunswick, NJ: Rutgers University Press, 2005) by Roger Finke and Rodney Stark explains how the "mainline" denominations lost their leadership of Christianity in America, how the Roman Catholic Church grew, and how the "upstart sects" like Baptists and Methodists became the dominant churches. Patrick Johnstone's *The Church Is Bigger Than You Think* (Pasadena, CA: William Carey Library, 1998) explains how evangelical churches are growing faster today than at any time in history. Patrick Johnstone and Jason Mandryk's *Operation World* (Waynesboro, GA: Paternoster, 2001) is an almanac of Christian presence in individual countries around the world.

The writings of Dietrich Bonhoeffer, Karl Barth, and many other theologians of the twentieth century remain widely available. While some of these will mightily test evangelical convictions, and some will prompt outright disgust, if you want to understand where the church is today, they are important to know. Bonhoeffer's *The Cost of Discipleship* will challenge the most dedicated Christian to rethink the Sermon on the Mount.

And there are many, many other resources out there to help you *continue* to think about church history. I hope you will. It'll make a difference in your own history.

Notes

1. J. Stevenson, *A New Eusebius* (London: S.P.C.K., 1963), 300.
2. For a full discussion of this see Ralph D. Winter and Bruce A. Koch, "Finishing the Task: The Unreached Peoples Challenge," *Perspectives on the World Christian Movement* 3rd ed., ed. Ralph D. Winters (Pasadena, CA: William Carey Library), 1999.

About the Author

DR. ROBERT DON (BOB) HUGHES is a lifelong Christian educator and writer. Born within a mile of the beach in California, he now teaches missions, evangelism, world religions, and apologetics at Clear Creek Baptist Bible College in Pineville, Kentucky. He spent two terms as a missionary in Africa, first in Zambia and then Nigeria. He regularly assists churches as interim pastor or revival leader. He's better known on the Internet as the author of such fantasy and science fiction novels as *The Prophet of Lamath* and *The Eternity Gene*.

He and his wife, Gail, live on the side of a mountain with a beautiful view toward the Cumberland Gap. His daughter, Bronwynn, an artist, lives and works in New York. Besides preaching, teaching, and writing, his primary interests are games of any kind, most especially college football.

Check out these other titles from the NavPress TH1NK Reference Collection.

Worldviews

ISBN-13: 978-1-57683-955-3
ISBN-10: 1-57683-955-9

In their search for answers to life's tough questions, people are adopting a range of conflicting worldviews. With a conversational style and refreshing perspective, this guide aims to provide a broad view of the origins and core beliefs of world religions and set them in context with the Christian faith.

Theology

ISBN-13: 978-1-57683-957-7
ISBN-10: 1-57683-957-5

When it comes to views of God, people seem to choose one of two perspectives: One group sees the Bible and our beliefs as black and white ideals; the other group views everything as gray. *Theology* honestly examines the beliefs Christians agree on while exploring the gray areas that divide them.

The Bible

ISBN-13: 978-1-57683-956-0
ISBN-10: 1-57683-956-7

Almost everyone agrees that daily Bible reading is an essential part of our walk with God. Inside this resource, you'll find answers to tough questions, essential biblical highlights, and individual reading plans that allow you to grow at your own pace.

To order copies, visit your local Christian bookstore, call NavPress at 1-800-366-7788, or log on to www.navpress.com.
To locate a Christian bookstore near you, call 1-800-991-7747.

Wake up to a new kind of quiet time.

7 Minutes with the Holy Spirit

ISBN-13: 978-1-57683-815-0
ISBN-10: 1-57683-815-3

Who is the Holy Spirit? Why is the Spirit so central to our lives? In 70 original readings from *The Message// Remix*, learn why a relationship with the Holy Spirit is essential.

7 Minutes with Jesus

ISBN-13: 978-1-57683-814-3
ISBN-10: 1-57683-814-5

Want to know Christ and make Him known? *7 Minutes with Jesus* allows you to zero in on His life and teachings with 70 short, daily readings.

7 Minutes with God

ISBN-13: 978-1-57683-813-6
ISBN-10: 1-57683-813-7

These insightful readings build your faith while culti-vating a lifetime habit of spending time with God each day. *7 Minutes with God* shows you that it's not only possible read the Bible every day, it's the best way to see more of their life from God's perspective.

To order copies, visit your local Christian bookstore, call NavPress at 1-800-366-7788, or log on to www.navpress.com.
To locate a Christian bookstore near you, call 1-800-991-7747.

Check out the Redefining Life series from NavPress!

With unflinching honesty and challenge, the REDEFINING LIFE series helps young adults in their early to mid twenties ask essential, life-defining questions that will characterize their lives from this point forward. Each of these practical studies includes readings from books, magazines, and The Message Bible designed to spark lively discussion and self-reflection. Go through the books on your own, or even better, get a group of friends and study them together. Gain insights on these and other topics from a biblical and current perspective.

Purpose

ISBN-13: 978-1-57683-827-3
ISBN-10: 1-57683-827-7

What makes the difference between merely being alive and really living? In this discussion guide you will be challenged to ask yourself some tough questions about your significance and where you find it.

Identity

ISBN-13: 978-1-57683-828-0
ISBN-10: 1-57683-828-5

There is freedom in knowing who you are, and this discussion guide will help with the process. You'll not only discover what you were created for but also learn about the One who created you.

Career

ISBN-13: 978-1-57683-887-7
ISBN-10: 1-57683-887-0

Redefining Life: My Career sets up realistic expectations of what you can anticipate in your new career: surviving a nerve-wracking interview, handling a prickly supervisor, and most important, representing Christ through it all.

Check out these other great titles from NavPress!

Memorize This

ISBN-13: 978-1-57683-457-2
ISBN-10: 1-57683-457-3

A specialized version of NavPress' successful *Topical Memory System*, this book will help you deal with whatever life throws at you. Get the Bible off your shelf and in your heart—where it belongs.

Left of Matthew

Norman Hubbard
ISBN-13: 978-1-60006-052-6
ISBN-10: 1-60006-052-8

The Old Testament chronicles God's relentless pursuit of His children and lays the foundation for a new covenant through Christ. *Left of Matthew* offers a fresh perspective for studying the Bible. This nine-week course explores key Old Testament themes—such as creation, sin, and the law—and connects them with New Testament truths. You'll discover the divine thread running through Scripture and see the Bible as one complete picture of God's love.

Right of Malachi

Norman Hubbard
ISBN-13: 978-1-60006-053-3
ISBN-10: 1-60006-053-6

Since the church began, the New Testament has been essential reading for believers. *Right of Malachi* offers a nine-week course that connects key New Testament themes with their origins in the Old Testament. You'll discover the eternal thread running throughout Scripture and view the Bible as one complete picture of God's love.

To order copies, visit your local Christian bookstore, call NavPress at
1-800-366-7788, or log on to www.navpress.com.
To locate a Christian bookstore near you, call 1-800-991-7747.

NAVPRESS⊘®